SWINGING INTO GOLF

by

ERNEST JONES

Professional, Women's National Golf and Tennis Club, Glenhead, N. Y.;
Formerly Professional at Chislehurst Golf Club,
Kent, England

and

INNIS BROWN

Golf Commentator and Formerly Managing Editor,
The American Golfer

Martino Publishing
Mansfield Centre, CT
2009

Martino Publishing
P.O. Box 373,
Mansfield Centre, CT 06250 USA

www.martinopublishing.com

ISBN-13: 978-1-57898-758-0 (hardcover: alk. paper)
ISBN-10: 1-57898-758-X (hardcover: alk. paper)
ISBN-13: 978-1-57898-759-7 (pbk.: alk. paper)
ISBN-10: 1-57898-759-8 (pbk.: alk. paper)

© 2009 Martino Publishing

Library of Congress Cataloging-in-Publication Data

Jones, Ernest, 1887-
Swinging into golf / by Ernest Jones and Innis Brown.
  p. cm.
Originally published: New York: Whittlesey House, 1937.
ISBN-13: 978-1-57898-758-0 (hardcover: alk. paper)
ISBN-10: 1-57898-758-X (hardcover: alk. paper)
ISBN-13: 978-1-57898-759-7 (pbk. alk. paper)
ISBN-10: 1-57898-759-8 (pbk.: alk. paper)
1. Golf. I. Brown, Innis. II. Title.

GV965.J57 2009
796.352--dc22   2009019062

Cover design by T. Matarazzo

Printed in the United States of America On 100% Acid-Free Paper

Further *demonstrations of precision and timing through swinging. Note coincidence of the club shaft and the weighted handkerchief at the bottom; also exact coincidence between the two, swung singly in the two hands above, the weight pulling the handkerchief perpendicularly upward.*

SWINGING INTO GOLF

by

ERNEST JONES

*Professional, Women's National Golf and Tennis Club, Glenhead, N. Y.;
Formerly Professional at Chislehurst Golf Club,
Kent, England*

and

INNIS BROWN

*Golf Commentator and Formerly Managing Editor,
The American Golfer*

New York WHITTLESEY HOUSE *London*

M c G R A W - H I L L   B O O K   C O M P A N Y ,   I N C .

PUBLISHED BY WHITTLESEY HOUSE
A division of the McGraw-Hill Book Company, Inc.

Printed in the United States of America by The Maple Press Co., York, Pa.

Dedicated to my good friend
MISS MARION HOLLINS
founder of the Women's National Golf
and Tennis Club

FOREWORD

CONTRARY to the experiences of Ernest Jones, I am not a practical golf teacher, but sixteen years' experience on the editorial staff of a golf magazine exposed me to countless theories about the game. Over that time I talked with hundreds of professionals and low-scoring amateurs, and likewise with several times as many so-called "duffers." These latter, though lacking the skill of the former, conceded nothing in their enthusiasm, nor yet in vivid imaginings in the field of theory.

I have listened to enthusiastic recitals of the discoveries of no end of "secrets" of good golf. In turn, I have been asked confidentially whether the professionals do not have some inner secret which they are pledged not to divulge to ordinary mortals. One is quite as ridiculous as the other. There is no "secret" to playing golf well any more than there is to throwing a baseball, or playing a piano, and so on.

Laying aside wild speculation, my most marked impression, drawn from these experiences, is the widely divergent ways in which those who actually play well themselves go about explaining how they do it to others. The situation is not unlike

the experiences of the six blind men who went to
see the elephant. Each is positive and emphatic
in his conception, however much it may differ
from the views of another, and taken all together
they are worth little in helping the beginner on his
way to a better game.

Out of it all, these three considerations seem to
me fundamental: First, the golf stroke, with all who
play consistently well, is basically a swinging
action. Second, one plays golf under the guidance
of the sense of touch or "feel" and not through
the sense of sight; one must learn to sense a
swinging action through feel. Third, where an
action is guided by feel, it must be subconsciously
controlled, in order to insure uniform performance.
Therefore, the most serious obstacle to be overcome
is the activity of the conscious mind in its tendency
to interrupt subconscious control. This situation, of
course, gives rise to statements frequently encountered on the importance of the mental phase of
playing the game.

Any method of teaching that squares with these
three principles is directed along sound lines.
Strictly speaking, the third principle has more to
do with the method of teaching than with the basic
conception of the stroke and how it is to be
produced, but it is identified so closely with any
effort at producing the stroke that it has been
included here with the other two.

Reasonably good form is essential to uniformly good performance in any field, and good form means the application of sound principles. There can be no permanent consistent improvement in a player's game except along these lines. Quick cures are likely to be quack cures. To play golf well requires learning a sound method of stroking the ball and reasonable application, either in play or in practice. Just how much one is willing to pay, in terms of time and effort, for what one gets is a matter of individual decision. The matter of chief concern should be that one gets what one actually pays for.

INNIS BROWN.

NEW YORK, N. Y.,
April, 1937.

INTRODUCTION

I BEGAN playing golf as a small boy, near Manchester, England. At the age of eighteen, I received the appointment as assistant professional at the Chislehurst Golf Club on my qualifications as a good club maker and good player. I played a very creditable game, good enough, in fact, to qualify each time I entered the British Open Championship, in which I took part several times.

One of my duties as professional was to teach others to play. From my first effort, I realized that I had not the slightest idea of how to go about it. The situation was about the same as though I were being sent out to teach people how to throw stones. I could throw with reasonable accuracy, just as I could play golf quite well, but what then?

Something had to be done, so I decided that my best course was to begin a careful study of books on the game and how to teach it. I read books by the leading professionals, and many others besides, but I am frank to confess that, with a single exception, these, instead of helping me, merely added to my confusion, because of their many contradictions.

There was among these a volume, "The Art of Golf" by Sir Walter Simpson, published in 1887, which proved very helpful because it set me to thinking along a line entirely different from anything I had encountered up to this time. It pointed out, among other things, that in golf "there is one categorical imperative, 'Hit the Ball,' but there are no minor absolutes."

This book emphasized the point that, while good players one and all, observe this one imperative, they differ, each from another, in the outward appearances of their actions. If that were true, then outward appearances were, after all, merely incidental. On that same theory, trying to teach golf by analyzing, bit by bit, successive movements in the stroke of a good player was an illogical procedure.

I still have a copy of "The Art of Golf," now long since out of print, and I treasure it highly. It marked the starting point for me in whatever success I have had at teaching the game. For that reason I hasten to give credit to it here and now.

Shortly after the outbreak of the World War, I joined the British army and was sent to France in November, 1915. In the fighting around Loos in March of the following year, I was badly wounded, and lost my right leg below the knee. Sent back to England, I was discharged from the hospital four months later. While still recuperating, I went back to golf. I was using crutches at the time, but in my first round I scored an 83 at Royal Norwich, and a bit later, playing with David Ayton, I scored 72 over the Clacton course, quite a long and testing layout.

I mention these personal experiences by way of showing that in spite of my physical handicap, which obviously must have changed the outward appearance of my stroke, I could still play well. This fact further confirmed me in my belief that the important essential in learning to play golf well is to accept the theory that the stroke must be regarded as one complete action, and to learn to put this theory into practice in wielding the club.

About this time I took part in several exhibition matches, and it was through these matches that I met Daryn Hammond, who wrote "The Golf Swing, the Ernest Jones Method," in which it was pointed out that the essence of the golf stroke is to have control of the club head through the hands and fingers. Twenty years of teaching this same principle has tended to prove and strengthen my faith in it. Playing golf is an art and not a science, and I have heard art defined as the science of elimination. So I have sought to eliminate other considerations and to stick to one principle, the art of swinging the club head.

I am speaking, of course, as a practical teacher. I have no quarrel with those who delight in analyzing the successive movements of different parts of the anatomy during the course of a stroke. Lots of us have a consuming curiosity to take a watch apart to see what makes it go. "The average golfer," to quote Sir Walter Simpson again, "must be allowed to theorize to some extent. It is a necessary concession to him as a thinking animal. . . . On the other hand, if he does not recognize hitting the ball as his main business, and theory as a recreation, he becomes so bad a player that he nearly gives it up."

I think "Swing the club head" is preferable to "Hit the ball" because there are more ways than one of hitting it; a detailed discussion of this point will be found later in the text. And I claim nothing new or revolutionary in "Swing the club head," because the identical term "swing" is used to designate the player's effort to wield the club, whether it bears any resemblance to a real swing or not. Yet I am convinced that very few players indeed can explain satisfactorily just what is meant by swinging the club head, and further that few high-handicap players really swing in making a stroke.

The above, then, sets forth my conception of the problem involved in teaching others to play. It sounds quite simple, and it is simple—so simple, in fact, that I find it difficult at times to get pupils actually to accept it. For this reason, it becomes necessary to resort to much repetition. If, in reading the text that follows, the reader feels that this is being overdone, I beg him to believe that I have not been able to bring about satisfactory results in any other way, after more than twenty years of seeking.

Good golf is easy to play, and easy golf is enjoyable golf. It is regrettable indeed that so many persons who play golf, or play at it, make such a labor of it. If through the message of instruction presented herein I can help even a small percentage of the great army of laborers at golf to become players, I shall feel highly repaid for my effort.

ERNEST JONES.

NEW YORK, N. Y.,
April, 1937.

CONTENTS

PART ONE
THE SWING TECHNIQUE
by ERNEST JONES

Contents

PART TWO

GENERAL OBSERVATIONS AND COMPARISONS OF THE JONES SYSTEM WITH OTHER METHODS

by INNIS BROWN

Part I

THE SWING TECHNIQUE

By ERNEST JONES

WHAT IT IS ALL ABOUT

FAULTY methods of doing a thing obviously add to the difficulties of satisfactory performance. And the difficulty that a great many thousands of people encounter in their efforts to learn to play a creditable and enjoyable game of golf stoutly implies serious faults in the methods they follow in trying to learn the game.

When one has gone along for some time doing a thing in an awkward, cumbersome manner, in order to learn the right way, it becomes necessary first to correct the existing faulty method. Therefore, before setting out to explain my own method of teaching, I want to point out wherein I feel most people make mistakes.

Briefly summed up, I think the fundamental difficulty lies in a negative instead of a positive approach; golfers start from a premise of trying to find out what is wrong when the shot does not come off satisfactorily, instead of getting back to the positive consideration of what it is that causes the shot to prove satisfactory. That this approach is a natural result of the system of teaching employed by their instructors is all the more unfortunate.

I know the old saying that "To know what is wrong is one way of knowing what is right," but I am afraid this is a long and circuitous route to follow in learning to play golf. There are too many wrong ways, when it comes to the matter of identifying these in detail, and the process of elimination in finding eventually what is right proves tedious and discouraging.

This consideration of details of wrong methods suggests the second fundamental difficulty in the approach to learning the game, namely, that of trying to take the stroke apart and identify it piece by piece through visual observation of what this or that good player appears to do as he plays a stroke. This means trying to learn the game solely through application of the sense of sight, whereas every good golfer in the world plays the game through the guidance of the sense of touch or feel.

I know any number of persons who can give you an excellent word picture of what actually takes place as a good player makes a stroke, but who are totally incapable of making a correct stroke

4

themselves. They have watched others, read articles analyzing their actions, and studied pictures of them in various stages of the stroke, until they have an accurate and correct picture of what the action should be, but they are quite incapable of producing the action. Granted that they have chosen excellent models, the basic mistake they make is the failure to realize that, whereas they are watching an expert perform, they are missing entirely the methods employed by the expert in reaching the estate of expertness.

This is quite illogical, because the expert never became expert by following a procedure of this kind. The skillful performer in any line made his start by acquiring a sense of the fundamentals involved. Consciously or subconsciously he acquired mastery of these fundamentals in their proper application, and gradually molded them into his own particular style of performance. It is for this reason that I insist the simplest way to learn golf is to get back to acquiring first an understanding of what it is the good player does consistently that the poor one does only occasionally, if at all.

Briefly stated, every good golfer displays *control*, *balance*, and *timing* in wielding the club. Without these factors no one becomes a consistently good player. Practically all discussions of the game from the instructive side abound in references to these

5

three points, but usually, when one presses for explicit, detailed explanation of just what is meant by any one or all, the answers received are vague and indefinite.

One hears, for instance, that this or that expert player has fine control. But just what is control, how is it achieved, and what does it mean? In brief, what are we trying to achieve in swinging a golf club? Now, questions on fundamentals of any subject frequently sound simple—so simple, in fact, as to appear ridiculous. The above question may strike the reader as just that. We are trying to strike the ball with the club head, of course. That's obvious, to be sure—so obvious that a great army of golfers, trying desperately to remember half a dozen things, or more, at the time of wielding the club, entirely forget the main purpose.

We are trying to strike the ball with the club head, so it should be plain that we must have control of the club head. Next, what are the dominant factors in the action of the club head in striking the ball? The answer to that is *speed* and *accuracy*. To get maximum distance from the effort, the club head must be traveling at the maximum speed at the instant of impact. So, also, the higher the speed, the finer the degree of accuracy in the well-made stroke, as I shall explain later on. We want maximum speed, and we want it at the right time and place—the instant of impact.

THE FIRST *four pictures above, from left to right, show a simple routine for arriving at a position of balance and freedom. First, stand comfortably erect and extend the arms at full length, with the palms of the hands facing; next, bring the hands together, with the right immediately above and touching the left; then*

*lower the hands into position on a vertical center line in
front of the body; finally close the fingers as in holding
the club. Easy body balance and balance between the two
hands result. The fifth figure is introduced to show one
position in which this balance has purposely been
destroyed by a deliberate effort with the hips.*

In approaching the factor of speed and how to attain it, let me first direct your attention to the action of a pendulum. On first consideration, the easy rhythmic movement of a pendulum, of an old-fashioned clock, let us say, back and forth, hardly suggests speed. But reflect a moment; if the arc through which the pendulum is swung is gradually increased, the pendulum must in time move through a complete circle. To move an object in a circular path, the power must be applied at the center. That is centrifugal application of power. It is one of two basic methods of applying power; the other is leverage. In wielding a golf club, one swings the club head with the hands around the center. Centrifugal application of power can and does develop the greatest speed possible from a given supply of power.

Now suppose we look at the movement of the club head in a golf stroke by comparison with the action of a pendulum. It does not matter how long or how short the stroke is; this is merely a matter of the size of the angle through which the pendulum or the club head is moved. No matter how large or how small this angle may be, the nature of the action remains the same and the movement of the club head is always under control. The speed of the movement is dependent on the amount of power applied, but the nature of the response is always uniform.

7

MOVING *a weight back and forth on the end of a string, in this fashion, is possibly the simplest demonstration of a swinging action. A pocketknife attached to the corner of a handkerchief serves the same purpose. Since the handkerchief is flexible, it cannot transmit power through leverage.*

A swinging action in moving the club head is the source of control in a golf stroke, and it is the only reliable and dependable source. Therefore we arrive at the conclusion that, in order to acquire control, we must learn to move the club head with a swinging action. This must be the chief aim, first, last, and all the time, if we are to acquire a positive and recognizable base on which to build in developing skill in playing golf. It is the one essential present in the stroke of every good golfer. A swinging action dominates the stroke of the experts, one and all, regardless of how different individuals may seem to vary one from another in outward appearance while playing a stroke.

The problem of how to acquire and apply control calls for much fuller discussion, to be taken up in later chapters. I want now to turn to a consideration of *balance*, second of the three basic factors. Balance is a state, a condition. It is simple and easily understood. When a person stands erect with his weight evenly distributed on his two feet, he displays a simple form of easy balance in a condition of rest or absence of movement. When he walks, he exhibits balance in motion. In either case he is a ready and simple exhibit of easy balance, maintained entirely without conscious thought or effort.

Balance in playing a golf stroke starts with a condition of rest, and develops into a condition of movement. In both phases it is quite as simple as in standing or walking, if we only cease to look at it as an end consciously to be attained. Only when we insist on considering it in the light of transfer

I T IS *possible to move the head of a golf club in a circular path, through the application of leverage, as this drawing shows. Very many golfers have gone on doing so for years, without learning what is meant by swinging the club head.*

of weight, as a matter for conscious effort, does balance become a perplexing and annoying problem. Obviously, then, we are dragging in unnecessary grief when we insist on thinking out a plan for keeping balanced as the club is moved first back, then forward. The simplest solution to such a problem is merely to put away any thought of trying consciously to maintain balance.

Bᴜᴛ *here is what happens when pressure or leverage is used in trying to cause the knife on the end of the handkerchief to move back and forth. The flexible medium cannot apply leverage.*

11

In swinging a golf club through any considerable arc, the body plainly must do a certain amount of turning. That changing of body posture destroys the condition of balance at rest, unless there is a compensating movement to maintain it. That identical situation is true in walking, yet no conscious thought is given to maintaining balance as you walk along under normal conditions over a fairly level or flat surface. When you walk uphill, you instinctively lean forward. You are maintaining your sense of balance in doing so, but you are quite unconscious of a definite purpose in doing so.

This is exactly what should take place in playing a golf stroke. All movement to maintain the condition of balance should be purely responsive to the main purpose of the action you are consciously trying to execute, that is, wielding the golf club. In no case should there be a conscious action aimed at maintaining balance as an end in itself. You cannot possibly achieve the two actions at the same time through conscious effort.

The main purpose in playing a golf stroke is to strike the ball with the club head. The hands hold and control the club. You try consciously to control this action through the use and movement of the hands. Maintaining the condition of balance must be responsive to what you are trying to do with your hands, just as it is when you swing a pair of Indian clubs, for example, or perform any of the

12

innumerable other physical acts common in everyday life. You cannot hope consciously to control what you are doing with the hands and at the same time to direct body contortions in an effort to maintain balance. You strike the ball with the club head and you control the club head through the manipulation of the hands, not through the conscious turning or twisting of the body. Forget the latter, and let it respond naturally to the main purpose, as it does in walking.

Coming now to *timing*, suppose we submit the simple question: Just what are you timing? Why, the striking the ball with the club head. Unless you can feel what you are doing with the club head, you cannot possibly have any idea or sense of timing. Expressed in one way, timing means producing the maximum speed with the club head at the instant of impact against the ball. From the standpoint of those who prefer to approach the problem of learning golf from the analytical angle of identifying the outward appearance of a correct stroke, timing might be defined as the proper coordination of body, arms, and hands to produce this maximum speed at the designated time. But I doubt that this is going to be very helpful to anybody in learning to develop timing in his own stroke.

Perfect timing is the identification of a true swinging action. It is the essence of rhythm, or

13

measured motion. If you swing a weight on the end of a string, the speed at which the weight can be made to move is proportional to the amount of force applied. Regardless of the speed at which the weight is moved, there is always a feel of the presence of the weight at the end of the string, exerting an outward pull on the source of application, due to the basic nature of centrifugal application. Throughout the movement there is complete coordination or uniformity between the amount of force applied and the result obtained in speed at which the weight is moved. Again, a swinging action is the only positive and reliable insurance for producing and maintaining this uniformity of relation. In other words, a true swing cannot fail to produce perfect timing.

Timing is a product of moving the club head with smooth rhythm. Consider, for instance, the case of a child jumping a rope. Coordination is achieved by centering the attention on the action of swinging the rope with the hands and not on the jumping. The swinging action with the rope lends itself to timing and rhythm, and the act of jumping is attuned to the swinging of the rope. Consider for a moment the difficulty of trying to reverse the procedure.

Let us review what has been said of the three essentials to a correct swing, control, balance, and timing. Control may best and most easily be

14

assured through the use of a swinging action in wielding the club. Furthermore, balance and timing are natural and logical adjuncts of swinging, which result without conscious action or thought on our part; these two factors become troublesome only when we set out to make them objectives of conscious effort.

Control, combining balance and timing, can be attained through developing a swinging action in wielding the club. We sense control through a feeling in the hands of what is being done with the club head. This, I submit, is a positive way to learn golf—to learn what we are doing when we are playing well, instead of worrying about what we are doing when we are playing badly. It affords a definite point of orientation. There can be little satisfaction to a traveler to be told that he is traveling a wrong road to reach an expressed destination, unless he is told also how to find the right road. Learn to swing the club head and to know when you are swinging; this is and for many years has been the basic theme in my teaching.

HOW TO HOLD THE CLUB

WE strike a golf ball with the head of the club, and we hold the club with the hands. It follows, therefore, that the method of holding the club must be of real importance. The manner of holding any tool or implement must obviously be suited to the way in which it is to be used, if the best results are to be obtained.

It is customary to refer to the manner in which the hands are placed on the club as the "grip." This is, I think, in a measure, unfortunate, because the word "grip" rather implies holding onto something with a viselike tensity. Such tensity is not needed in holding a golf club; furthermore, it will prove a serious obstacle to wielding the club properly. However, since the term is in common

16

usage, it will be used here, but with the reminder that it applies only to the position of the hands as they are placed on the club.

There are three general types of grip, each referring to a specific disposition of the two hands in their relation each to the other. These are the *overlap*, the *interlock*, and the so-called *natural*. In the first, the thumb of the left hand extends diagonally across the shaft, and the pad of the thumb of the right hand rests on it, while the little finger of the right hand is lapped over the forefinger of the left. In the second, the thumb of the left hand extends across the shaft back of the right, while the little finger of the right and the forefinger of the left are interlocked. In the natural grip, the two hands are free from any interlocking or overlapping, the fingers of one hand occupying relatively the same positions on one side of the shaft as those of the other hand do on the reverse side.

Each method has had its exponents among the winners of great championships, although very few players today are to be found using the natural method. I strongly favor and recommend the overlap method for one very important reason, namely, the positions of the thumbs and first fingers of the two hands. These members are of tremendous importance in sensing a feel of the club head, and I consider it necessary that they both have actual contact with the shaft.

17

Realizing the difficulty of creating word pictures that will leave no doubt of the correct method of placing the hands, I am introducing several photographs and drawings, which show plainly and unmistakably just how the hands are to be placed; thus the rest of this discourse will be devoted to explaining the aim we are trying to attain. In studying the pictures, the reader is asked to keep in mind at all times that the same principle guides one in holding a golf club that applies in the holding of other tools and implements. That is, hold it just securely enough to assure control of it throughout the action.

Let us consider, for example, the holding of a pen for writing. The expert penman holds it just tightly enough to guide it lightly over the surface of the paper. There is no need to clutch it, because the action is not such as to demand it. Gripping a pen quite tightly destroys flexibility and dexterity and merely makes writing difficult. So also with tight gripping in golf. The power for tight gripping is exercised through the back of the hands, and is highly useful in delivering a heavy blow. But in golf the aim is to deliver a swift blow and not a heavy one. There is a distinct difference between the two.

The thumbs and forefingers do not have so much power for gripping but they, particularly the thumb, enjoy a much wider latitude of movement and are, therefore, the leading factors in directing

18

the movement of the club. Also, since speed in wielding the club is a main consideration, it follows that the club is held and wielded largely with the fingers and not with the palm of the hand. For

THE PALM *side of the left hand showing the correct relation of the thumb to the forefinger.*

A FRONT *view of the thumb and forefinger of the left hand, showing relation of thumb and forefinger.*

instance, in throwing a stone one holds it chiefly in the fingers, but in laying hold of a rope for a tug or war one holds it in the palms. In golf the club is held in the hand with the fingers. A study of the pictures shows correct position.

In the matter of the relation of the hands, the illustrations show that they are placed so as to face each other squarely. That is to say, if you extend the left arm straight out in front of the body at full length with the palm turned in, then raise the right up to where it just touches the left, also with the palm turned in, and then lower both hands to the approximate position they hold in addressing the ball, you will have the two in the correct positions relative to each other.

This is a "balanced" position, and is entirely logical for the purpose to be served. Thus, if you were to bounce a ball off the floor, the palm of the hand would face straight down; if you were to bounce it against the ceiling, the palm would face squarely upward. In making a golf stroke, the movement is first in one direction and then in the reverse. The hand must, therefore, be placed so as to make movement in each direction equally easy and comfortable.

Reference to the "balance" in hand position, as shown in the pictures, will reveal that the thumb and forefinger on each hand have identical positions on reverse sides of the shaft. This is as it should be to facilitate swinging. Yet I realize that the reader may be ready to point out that he has observed this or that well-known player who departs radically from this position, and he will, of course, be quite right in his observation.

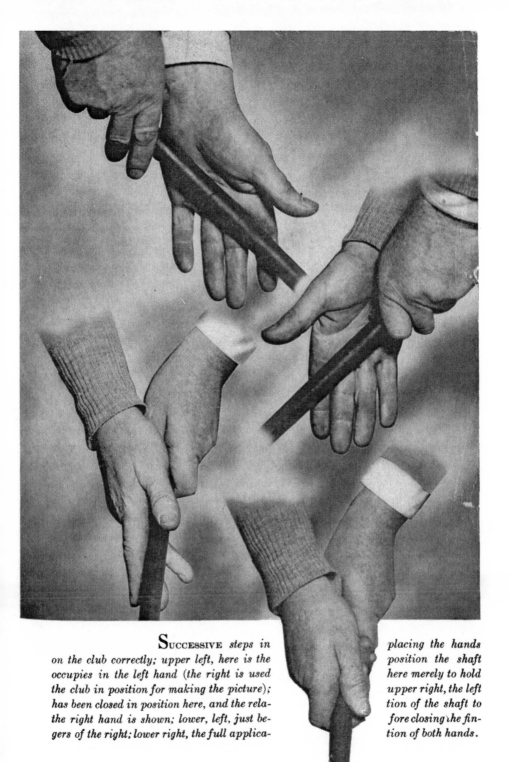

Successive *steps in* placing the hands *on the club correctly; upper left, here is the* position the shaft *occupies in the left hand (the right is used* here merely to hold *the club in position for making the picture);* upper right, the left *has been closed in position here, and the rela-* tion of the shaft to *the right hand is shown; lower, left, just be-* fore closing the fin- *gers of the right; lower right, the full applica-* tion of both hands.

CORRECT *hand position is important, so that the two hands may work in as full unison as possible. The palms of the two face squarely toward each other, in a balanced position. Both thumbs extend diagonally across the shaft, clasping it between the thumb and forefinger.*

21

But let me say this: I know many fine golfers who play beautiful golf in spite of the handicap of faulty gripping. They happen to have learned that way, and any other method would for the time being feel distinctly awkward if they chose to make a change. At the same time we are aiming at simplifying the game as far as possible, and certainly there is no better place to start than in adopting the right method of holding the club. It will save more than a little grief later on.

Before moving on to consideration of other phases, let me add just a few more words on the amount of tension to be employed in holding the club. It has been my observation that far more high handicap players err through gripping too tightly than through loose gripping; yet laxness in holding the club must be avoided. See that you hold it securely enough to maintain full control throughout.

I have frequently been asked whether or not there should be a loosening of the grip as the club gets to its maximum position in the back-swing, in order to allow for ease and freedom in changing the direction in the movement of the club head. Possibly the reader has seen very good golfers do this. But if they did, it was not by design, and in all probability they were not even aware that they did it. A firm, secure hold on the club should be maintained right through the stroke from start to finish.

HOW TO STAND TO THE BALL

JUST as the manner in which the hands are placed on the club is of great importance in aiding an easy swinging action, so is the way one stands to the ball important in an easy response on the part of the body to the action of swinging. The position that the feet occupy in relation to each other and also to the location of the ball fixes the foundation on which the action of the stroke is carried out. Plainly, therefore, the character of the foundation will have much to do with the nature of that action.

As in the case of the grip, observation of any considerable number of successful players will reveal quite a range of difference in the matter of stance or the method of placing the feet. By common practice, three general types of stance are recognized—*open*, *square*, and *closed*. The term in each case refers to the position of the feet as related to the ball and the proposed line of play.

The square stance predominates. It finds the toes of the two feet in a line approximately parallel with the line of play. The open method finds the left foot drawn somewhat back from this line; the stance is called closed when the left foot is advanced nearer the line.

People play good golf using any one of the three. Thirty years or so ago the tendency in England was toward the closed stance. Then along came J. H. Taylor, who stood quite open and won several championships with that method, and straightway it became popular to employ an open stance. In more recent years most of the well-known players came to stand practically square. Within the past few years certain well-known players in this country profess to find particular merit in closing the stance again.

I mention these facts merely to point out that good golf may be played by using any one of the three, and that the simple device of adopting either, because it is strongly advocated or recommended by this player or that, can hardly be relied on to bring about any permanent improvement in a player's game, except in very rare cases. One

24

sees both good and bad golf played with all three types.

It is my feeling that the square method is the most logical and effective, and this is the method that I use and recommend. I do so because I think it provides true balance and also lends itself easily and readily to a free turn of the body in both directions, toward the right on the backswing and toward the left in the downswing. The closed method leaves the body in position for an easy turn in the backswing, but offers restraint in the downswing. The reverse is, of course, true where the stance is open. Players who see fit to depart from the square methods usually do so, after they appear to get better results in their own case, through a process of trial and error in working out adjustments of their swings.

I hope it is evident from the foregoing that the type of stance is not significant; until the player has made enough progress at the game to qualify at adjusting refinements in his play, he will do well to go along with the square position, for there are other things of importance to consider. Fundamentally, the stance should provide a feeling of ease and comfort. The posture should allow the body to yield easily to the action of swinging, with a minimum of tenseness and resistance. As one stands to the ball to begin the business of swinging, there should be a feeling of easy balance. That is to say, the player should feel balanced from side to side and likewise from back to front. It should be just as though he were standing easily erect with the two arms dropped at the sides, in the first preliminary stage. Placing the club head back of the ball will call for his bending forward slightly at the waist, but proper balance will prevent any surging forward on to the toes. The legs should be practically straight at the knees, but with a feeling of easy relaxation in these joints. They should never be stiff or rigid.

Avoid any effort at digging the feet into the ground, as if to engage in a weight-lifting contest or a tug of war. Such a procedure sets up a feeling of tenseness in the legs, which will be communicated to other parts of the body; this is distinctly hostile to the easy freedom needed for launching a swinging action. Aim at acquiring the easy freedom that accompanies a simple physical exercise, such, for instance, as one feels on the dance floor just at the instant of picking up the timing of the music to start dancing.

There is no scale of measurement to determine the necessary distance between the two feet, but roughly the width of the stance should be about that of the shoulders. Too wide a stance will restrict the action of the body, while placing the feet too closely together restricts the base of action and tends to disturb balance. Ordinarily the toes should be pointed so as to form an angle of approximately 45 degrees. From time to time one hears of some well-known player who has discovered special merit in standing with the toe pointed slightly inward. This may serve some purpose, but it is not clear to me what it is.

As to the distance one should stand from the ball, clearly the length of the club chosen for the stroke must be a factor. But in any case it is important to bear in mind that the position of the feet is to be determined by first placing the club head in position back of the ball and then adjusting the position, never by taking a position and then adjusting the swing to fit.

It has been suggested above that a slight bend at the waist is necessary to permit the player to take a starting position for the stroke. The prevailing error is toward bending over too much. The body ought to be kept reasonably erect, and, once the position is established, it should be maintained throughout the swing. Straightening up or bending lower cannot but destroy the effectiveness of the stroke.

The keynote to a smoothly timed stroke is a feeling of relaxation* and freedom from tenseness. If there is tenseness either in the hands and arms

---

* I would caution the reader as to the exact meaning intended by the words "relax" and "relaxation," which are used because they have come to be so common in discussions of golf. As used here, "relaxation" means "easy composure," not a condition bordering on inertness, or limpness.

or in the legs, it will absolutely forestall a swinging action at the start. This prompts me to say a few words about waggling, or the preliminary movement of the club head back and forth over the ball. A few movements of this kind are helpful. They allow the body to relax, and help to provide a feel of the club head. But excessive waggling may become a habit, and an objectionable one. In such a case the practice is probably more harmful than helpful.

The accompanying photographs and drawings will help the reader to identify more readily the correct way to take up a position, and a careful study of them is recommended.

A SWING AND HOW TO
ACQUIRE IT

UP to this point we have been concerned with pointing out that the basis of good golf is a swinging action, and with describing the methods of holding the club and placing the feet which lend themselves most readily and comfortably to developing and producing such an action. We come now to a consideration of how to acquire that action.

I approach the task with full realization of the difficulties of explaining it in terms that cannot be misunderstood, because it involves describing something that one must feel, and not something that one identifies through sight. It is simple enough to examine an action photograph of any expert player, to point to the position of this or that member of the body, and to explain how these different positions conform with a swinging action. But I have already explained why I think such a practice is of little value in the practical problem of teaching others to play well.

Even at the expense of repetition, then, let me say again that the good golfer has a feel of what he is doing with the club head. He does not see the successive movements that different parts of his anatomy execute through the stroke. Moreover, he never learned to play well through thinking or giving conscious consideration to the working of these different parts, other than to learn how to hold the club properly and how to stand correctly to the ball.

Let me begin by calling attention to the fact that swinging is a definite action in itself, and subject to its own peculiar laws. It is entirely free of, and distinct from, leverage. Swinging and levering are diametrically opposed methods of applying power. In a swing the connecting medium between the power and the object swung has both ends moving always in the same direction; in levering, the two ends of the medium move always in opposite directions. It is no more possible to join up the two in one unified application of power than it is to mix oil and water.

Here again, I think, photographs can be used to advantage to convey the right idea to the reader. I want first to direct your attention to the pictures

30

THE TEST of a true swinging movement. First is the movement back and forth of a pocketknife attached to the corner of a handkerchief. Then swinging both a club and the weighted handkerchief together, so that the movement of the two synchronize. Only through a true swing can this be accomplished. Leverage will not cause the weight on the handkerchief to respond in this way.

between pages 30 and 31. I am using here a device familiar to all to whom I have ever given personal instruction, and my constant companion in that kind of work—a pocket knife attached to one corner of a handkerchief, a convenient example of a weight on the end of a string. Examine first pictures 1 and 2. These show the action at opposite extremes, when the knife is swung through approximately half a circle. Observe that the handkerchief is drawn taut, because a swinging action is always an expanding action, with the weight exerting an outward pull.

I would suggest that the reader rig up a similar device of weight and string and try the experiment for himself, guiding the movement entirely through a feel of what is happening with the weight. As long as the weight is being swung, it will keep the string pulled taut, and this condition will prevail whether the swing be short or long.*

Examine next pictures 4 and 5. Here I am holding a club along with the handkerchief, executing a swing through approximately half a circle. The handkerchief in its movement serves as a check on whether there is an actual swing of the club head. If I push or pull on the shaft of the club, it may still be moved through a similar arc, but the move-

---

* Galileo discovered isochronism of the pendulum in 1581 by observing that the swinging lamps in the Cathedral of Pisa took the same time to complete the arc through which they swung, regardless of the distance they were suspended from the ceiling.

ment of the knife and the handkerchief will not coincide. Leverage, replacing swinging, may produce a result that appeals to the eye as being quite similar, because the shaft of the golf club is stiff and therefore a suitable medium for levering. But you cannot apply leverage through a highly flexible medium, such as a string or handkerchief.

I should like to emphasize again the fact that feel of the action, and not seeing it, is the necessary essential to its correct understanding, as the above experiments demonstrate. It requires something of an experienced eye to detect at once the difference between a true swinging movement, in moving the head of a golf club through the arc shown in these pictures, and the result that may be attained in a movement brought about through levering. The casual observer may be unable to detect any difference. But the check afforded by moving the club and the string with a weight on the end together is complete and convincing. Furthermore, continued experimentation with this test will finally enable the player to distinguish between the two methods, not only by the sense of sight but by a vastly more important method, so far as learning golf is concerned—that of feeling the difference.

The action demonstrated in these pictures is, of course, that of a pendulum. Its fundamental and distinguishing characteristic is the same whether

32

the pendulum is swung through a small arc or a large one. The maximum arc is a complete circle, assuming that the power is applied at a fixed center. The golf stroke actually is not a circle, because the center of the stroke, which is the center of gravity of the body, is not fixed throughout the stroke. At the same time the characteristic action of the pendulum is present throughout. No one makes an absolutely perfect swinging action in his golf stroke, but the more nearly he approaches a perfect swing, the steadier and the more consistent the results will be.

"Yes," says one, "all that you have said may be true, and I understand you when you say 'Swing the club head,' but I still do not understand exactly what you mean by 'swinging.' It is clear enough that, when you whirl a weight on the end of a string, you are swinging it, but I don't see just how this kind of swing can be made to coincide with a movement that has to change direction."

Suppose we go back to the pendulum again. One may readily picture a pendulum being swung through an arc of, let us say, 135 degrees, or three-quarters of a half circle. So also with a weight on the end of a string. But possibly it occurs to the objector, from experience of observation, that, if the swing is expanded to 180 degrees or a little beyond, a jerky or uneven action may result just at the instant when the change of direction is effected, although no such condition would develop in the action of whirling a weight through a complete circle.

However, a little reflection will reveal that the same agency which enables the person, swinging a weight on the end of a string through less than half a circle, to expand the arc conveniently to a complete circle without physical hindrance also makes possible the change in direction in the path traveled by the club head, without interference with the characteristic quality of swinging. This agency is flexible wrists, or, more properly, the unified action of the two wrists.

The wrists supply a factor in swinging a golf club that is impossible in a purely mechanical device, for, whereas the arms are in part stiff and rigid, they are also in part flexible. This flexibility in the wrists makes it possible for the golfer both to extend the arc of the swing and to bring about a change in direction without disturbing the rhythmic action characteristic of swinging. A sense of feel of what is being done with the club head takes care of this.

Identifying the correct action of the club head through the sense of touch or feeling is, therefore, the goal for which we are striving. And it is necessary that this feeling be sensed from the very start of action in beginning a stroke. Unless the stroke starts as a swinging action, there is but slight possibility that such action can or will be developed later on. The start is very important, which suggests the thought that probably every golfer at some time or other has found himself pondering over just how the movement should be started.

I have no thought of going into detailed analysis of the movements of different parts of the body in this or any other connection, but I do want to suggest that the answer to this question is quite simple in the light of what has been said about swinging. In producing a swing, the contact at the end of the medium, which transmits the power to whatever is being swung, initiates and guides the action. That is to say, in the case of a right-handed golfer, the left hand is at the end of the shaft, and therefore initiates and directs the movement. The reverse is true with left-handed players.

Understand that golf is neither a right-handed nor a left-handed game, but a two-handed one. Otherwise we should play it with either one hand or the other, as we do in tennis, for example. But so long as two hands are used, the one at the end of the shaft remains fixed throughout, and therefore is the guiding and directing agency. The same is true, of course, in wielding an ax or swinging a heavy hammer. For a right-handed person, the left retains a secure hold throughout, whereas the right may slide up and down the handle.

35

In a sense, the shaft of the club is an extension of the left arm, connecting the club head with the left shoulder, or at least forming the line between the two, used in transmitting the power from its source in the body to the club head. The hand, being the extremity of sensitivity in this power line, acquires and transmits the feel of the club head. The sensation, felt in the hands, of what is being done with the club head, is the guide by which conscious effort should be directed. All other physical actions on the part of the body should follow as responsive movement.

So much, then for suggestion on conscious physical effort in starting the stroke. Mental preparation for the start is just as important, possibly even more so. Chief concern here lies in the problem of physical tenseness, brought about by the mental condition that the player is experiencing at the time. Tenseness is an unsurmountable barrier to swinging, because swinging implies a free, easy rhythm, which can never be achieved in the face of tenseness. To detect tenseness, let me suggest the following simple experiment.

Hold the club between the thumb and first finger of one hand. Swing the head back and forth, gradually increasing the arc as far as this thumb-and-finger hold will permit. There should be no difficulty whatever in recognizing a feel of the swinging movement of the club head. Now, hold

36

the club with both hands, and resume the movement back and forth. So long as you retain a "feel" of the swinging action of the club, you will observe that the body is moving easily to accommodate the action of the hands and arms. You will recognize complete freedom from any tenseness or strain in any part of the body. There will be tension, in the sense that you feel the "pull" outward of the club head, just as you do in whirling a weight on a string. But there will be no tenseness, in the sense that some part of the body is setting up a resistance to a natural physical response by the body in giving to the action of swinging. Developing of such a resistance interrupts and destroys real swinging action.

The two simple experiments which I have suggested that the reader try for himself, that just above and the one where he is asked to hold both a golf club and a weight on the end of a string, are the most effective devices I can offer for helping him to learn to know and to identify a swing by feel; he must learn it in this way to make any lasting progress in learning to play golf well. The distinction I have drawn between the mechanics of swinging and levering will, I hope, help clarify his understanding of just what is meant by swinging. But he must go further than that. He must learn to know a swing by its feel, and no one can exercise his sense of touch or feel for him.

Were it possible to convey this message of swinging unfailingly through written words, there would be no need for anything further. However, I am not so optimistic as to hope for such a result. In the first place, I know from long practical experience that a great deal of time and patience is needed to get the message over, even when I have the pupil in hand and am, therefore, able to use personal example and demonstration. Since this is not possible in delivering the message in writing, I pass, therefore, to further consideration of the basic idea from somewhat varied points of view.

TIMING AND RHYTHM

FREQUENTLY I am confronted with the statement that any one knows you have to swing the club head, but that to play good golf, you have to do a lot more than that. As a matter of fact, you do not have to do more than learn to swing the club head in order to strike the ball the most forceful and yet the most accurate blow possible with the power at your command.

You can develop the maximum force at your command by developing club-head speed in swinging to strike the ball, but you cannot force a swing. I suspect that the latter idea is what persons have in mind when they say you have to do more than just swing the club head. I have spoken already of timing, and I have also made reference to rhythm. I have shown how we attempt to time the stroke

USE THE HANDS TO WIELD THE CLUB HEAD AND

TO SENSE CONTROL OF WHAT IS BEING DONE

WITH IT FROM FIRST TO LAST. ACTIONS BY

As an aid to grasping the theme of swinging the club head with the hands, the artist has omitted body outline in this series of sketches. You control the movement of the club head with the hands

40

OTHER BODY MEMBERS ARE RESPONSIVE ONLY TO

THIS CONSCIOUS PURPOSE OF MAINTAINING

CONTROL OF THE CLUB THROUGHOUT THE STROKE.

and you sense control through feel. Body positions at successive stages of the stroke are results of the action of swinging the club head, and are not striven for consciously by the player while wielding the club.

41

through a feeling of what we are doing with the club head in striking the ball. Furthermore I have asserted that, to do this most effectively, it is necessary to *swing* the club head. And perfect swinging is perfect rhythm.

I once heard a golfer who had followed Bobby Jones through a round of eighteen holes say that he could not identify a single thing that this great golfer did in playing a stroke. Every shot, he added, appeared to be so simple and so easy. And I once heard Miss Joyce Wethered, for whom I have a warm admiration, both for her charming personality and for her ability to play golf so beautifully, say that she had learned a great deal from Mr. Jones by observing his timing and rhythm.

These two observations are most interesting. An expert player herself, Miss Wethered knew and could appreciate that what made Mr. Jones's game seem so effortless was the smooth rhythmic way in which he swung the club. The other observer, bent on discovering and identifying this or that single movement or maneuver, to which he might attribute his subject's fine success, entirely overlooked the most essential thing of all—rhythmic smoothness in the stroke.

It is a characteristic of centrifugal application of power, that is, swinging, to appear effortless in its performance. There is no appearance of strain, so evident in levering. A giant wheel spun at a rate of 1,000, 2,000, or more revolutions per minute, may still give no hint of the terrific force driving it because this force is applied evenly and smoothly. But if, unfortunately, a flaw in its construction should result in its flying apart under the force, parts of it may be thrown a great distance and great damage may be done. The power driving a perfectly functioning wheel is there all right, but the method of its application does not readily suggest the force, measured by the results obtained. Likewise, in applying human power in swinging a golf club, the smoother and more rhythmic the swing, the less one is likely to suspect the range of the power solely from watching its application. But the results show in what happens to the ball.

Where fine timing and rhythm exist, there is not only little outward show of the real application of power but also an absence of any feeling of taxing physical effort. This, I think, explains the fact that a great army of golfers do such a deal of straining and surging in their efforts to hit the ball. I am convinced that a very large percentage of these have never in their golfing experiences actually felt the sensation of striking the ball with a real swing. Certainly efforts of this kind make hard physical labor of the game, though it should be no more than light exercise.

I had an excellent illustration of this point in my indoor school during the past winter. A very well-

43

known player came in for instruction. I said, "Of course, there can't be very much the matter with you; the trouble with you good players is that you are always trying to find out why you hit a shot badly, instead of learning to understand what it is you do when you hit one well."

"Well, to tell the truth," he said, "sometimes when I am playing well it seems so easy it is actually disappointing."

Exactly, and there is the rub. It was disappointing because, to him, the freedom of timing and rhythm were not recognizable. He had an instinctive feeling that something was lacking, yet by his own admission he was getting highly satisfactory results, playing his best game. Inability to sense timing and rhythm in the stroke, and thus establish a guide toward which he could always turn when for any reason his game began to go bad, left him a victim of worry over what was causing him to go wrong. Once you have learned to sense the feel of timing and rhythm embodied in a real swing, you will always have a definite base on which to check. Without it, you must go on groping in the dark.

If the reader happens to be one of the vast army to whom the game has thus far been largely an exhibition of grunting and groaning, may I suggest the possibility that he has at sometime, purely by accident, struck the ball with a real swing without knowing it. Doubtless he has had the experience of

44

purposely trying to play short of a hazard, when he struck the ball more or less lazily and with little conscious effort, only to see it travel considerably further than he expected, and maybe land plump in the hazard.

What happens in such cases is that the club is actually swung. The urge usually present to knock the ball a long way is missing. The club is moved in a more or less leisurely manner, free from the strain of conflicting movement usually set up through a process of leverage. A fuller discussion of the causes of these conflicting movements will be taken up in a later chapter. But I have brought in here brief mention of the matter, by way of emphasizing the great importance of timing and rhythm.

In line with what has been said of these elements in the swing and the importance of learning to sense their presence in the stroke, I want to make it plain that the player should swing the club head in a manner to produce them. This is distinct from any idea that the club head swings itself. Nothing would be more absurd than this latter. Yet it has come to me that I teach letting the club head swing itself. The club head must be moved with a swinging action, and the player must produce that action, through a feel of what he is doing with the club head with his hands.

Timing is felt in the motion of the club head. Correct timing is most easily and readily attained through a swinging action. A real swing is truly rhythmic in its nature. In striking a ball with a stick, or bat, or whatnot, correct timing is an absolute essential to satisfactory performance. When the ball is stationary, as in golf, and when no quick change of position by the player, to attain a striking position, is needed, a swinging action can be developed to its full advantage in producing both speed and precision in striking. Swing!

OBSTACLES TO SWINGING

A SENSE of rhythm and smoothness seems to be more highly developed in some persons than in others. Since rhythm is a fundamental characteristic of a swinging movement, this offers a plausible explanation of the greater difficulty encountered by some in learning to swing than by others. Also, I am inclined to believe that women as a rule are somewhat quicker at sensing the action with a golf club than men.

Probably this is because, from early childhood, boys are more accustomed to playing outdoor games than girls. Many of these games employ and develop the application of leverage. I have noticed, for instance, that oarsmen, in particular, generally find it difficult to develop a swinging stroke in golf. Their experience in rowing has been that of using

THERE *is an exact parallel between the action of swinging a golf club head with the hands and a child swinging in an old-fashioned swing. In both cases, the start is made slowly with a gradual increase in the application of power to develop speed.*

Tʜᴇ *"teeter" or seesaw of childhood days exemplifies the principle of leverage, where the two ends of the medium conveying the power move in opposite directions and the characteristic action in applying the power is quick and jerky.*

leverage. Similar tendencies, though hardly so marked, can frequently be detected in working with cricketers, baseball players, and tennis players.

But regardless of natural aptitude, or a possible heritage from one's experience at other games, there are always certain troublesome factors to be reckoned with. When a golfer steps up to his ball to play a stroke, where distance is a primary consideration, his purpose naturally is to knock it as far as he can. That means to hit it as hard as he can. (Make note of the use of that word "hit.") There is a subconscious urge to use all the power possible. This urge is quite instinctive, but it usually leads to trouble because of the manner in which he tries to apply the power.

The trouble arises from the mental conception he has of hitting the ball. In a sense it is unfortunate that we have become accustomed to the use of the word "hit" in referring to the impact of the club head against the ball, just as I have pointed out earlier that the use of the term "grip" to refer to the manner of holding the club may be misleading. So suppose we take a look at "hitting" in the light of its definition.

The dictionaries define "hitting" as "bringing into violent contact." The synonymous term "striking" is defined as "touching with some force"; also as "giving a blow to." Violence, in a discernible degree, is expressed in "hitting."

50

Violence implies or suggests suddenness, quickness. These are not necessarily implied in "striking." The distinction between the two terms does not involve the amount of force applied so much as it does the manner of its application. It is the manner of the application that is important, representing as it does the difference between swinging and levering, between a sudden, hurried attempt to exert power and a smooth rhythmic one.

There are, to be sure, more ways than one to strike a ball. You can strike it by swinging the club head or by employing leverage. You can strike it harder with a swinging action than you can in any other way with the power at your command, and still retain reasonable control over your effort. The principle of centrifugal application of force guarantees this. But it is not likely that you will come to a realization of this of your own accord. To do so is not consistent with your past experiences. Your natural instinct is to try to turn the power on all at once.

A swinging action must begin smoothly and rhythmically, and the force producing it must be applied gradually. There can be no quick jerky movement at any stage of the procedure. As soon as the movement develops this characteristic, the swinging action is destroyed. Steadiness, not speed, is the keynote in beginning the application of the power in a swing. Speed is developed later.

51

When the player begins the stroke with a mental purpose, however vague, of "hitting," as it has been defined already, subconsciously he tries to make a quick application of the power. As a consequence, he applies it at some intermediate point along the line of communication between the source (that is, the center of gravity of the body) and the other end of the line (that is, the club head). This, as has been pointed out, is quite impossible in an actual swing. It is as though, while swinging a weight on the end of a string with one hand, he attempted to increase the speed of the weight by pressing on the string with the other hand, say half way between the swinging hand and the weight.

Such a start can result only in a levering action, in which certain parts of the body are set to work at a contrary purpose to other parts, for leverage always finds the two ends of the medium moving in opposite directions. Visible results of this sort of thing are familiar to all of us. One very common form of the malady is to be seen in the chap who pulls his left foot back from its normal position, with nearly all his weight supported on the right leg at the finish of the stroke. An awkward unbalanced position at the finish is positive proof of the use of leverage in wielding the club.

Almost invariably a hurried jerky start in getting the club back travels hand in hand with trouble of this kind. But it is not enough merely to aim at starting the club slowly and deliberately. Such a practice may cut down the damage. But a slow start will avail little if the player is contending against conflicting forces. Leverage is leverage, whether it happens to be exemplified by the slow prying of a heavy object with a strong iron bar or by the faster wielding of a golf club.

In like manner, a swing is a swing, whether it be long or short. It always has its own peculiar distinguishing characteristics: the force applied at the center; the object swung always exerting an outward pull; and so on. These characteristics are recognizable by anyone who has learned to identify them through the sense of feel. A player is free to swing just as fast as he can, so long as he knows from the sensation relayed through feel with his hands that he is maintaining a real swinging action with the club head.

The foregoing may, I suppose, be called difficulties of natural impulse. They are born of the basic urge to apply all available power for knocking the ball as far as possible, and they are schooled in experience with other applications of physical power. They would be entirely reasonable difficulties in the case of a person who might try to hit a ball with a club the first time he saw one.

But there are other sources of difficulty, deriving from an entirely different background, which prove serious hindrances to thousands of golfers.

I refer now to the obstacles that the player sets up through trying to imitate the style of another, or, I might better say, through imitating certain outward appearances of some player whom he has chosen as a pattern or model. In the first place, the chances are that the observer has chosen for imitation certain actions that are no more than mannerisms at best. They are, in all probability, quite incidental, and of little or no importance. Dozens of these have been picked up, and elaborately explained in so-called instructive treatises on the game as a basic keynote to the skill exhibited by the player in question. I hardly need add that any such contention is pure rot.

Furthermore, if the observer is fortunate enough to identify and interpret correctly the movements of one or more parts of the body essential in swinging the club, he still has little, if any, chance of using his observation to advantage in improving his own play by consciously trying to reproduce the outward physical appearance of it. To do this is to fail to realize that this outward appearance is in reality quite incidental, so far as his model is concerned, to the important business of swinging the club head. This is the vital thing in the stroke, regardless of when and how the model acquired it.

Rest assured that the expert has never in any case developed his stroke into a swinging action by giving any conscious thought to the many different details with regard to what the different parts of his anatomy were doing. Remember, too, that the observer is watching the expert perform after the latter has attained the state of expertness. And in all likelihood he is forgetting the important matter of how expertness was attained. If you watch a skillful player perform merely in order to enjoy the artistry he displays, it is enough to dwell on the outward appearance of his style. But if you are trying to improve your own game, go back to the formula by which he developed his artistry.

Watching a great runner in action or a clever dancer rarely suggests his infancy, when he was learning to walk. Yet as a baby this expert had to lay the foundation for his later superb skill by the slow, laborious process of acquiring a feeling of balance in placing one foot before another. That was the groundwork, and without it, of course, there could have been no progress toward his becoming expert in his particular line.

No golfer should concern himself with trying consciously to copy the playing form of another, once he has reached an age when his inclination is to analyze action in terms of different movements. Fifty years ago Sir Walter Simpson wrote: "For you or me to model ourselves on a champion is about as profitless as to copy Hamlet in the hope of becoming a Shakespeare." That statement was true then, and it is true now. Expert players differ in their swings even as they do in the way they walk. Among all the golfers I have ever seen, I

55

would hesitate to say that I had ever seen any two who swing exactly alike. Yet the basic principles are the same for all in swinging a golf club, even as they are in walking.

"Yet," says one, "I have frequently heard it said that certain young players swing almost exactly like their teachers."

That may be true. I have known a great many players whose style reflected that of older players who had come under their observation while they were learning. But don't accept that fact as a rebuttal to the advice against avoiding any effort to copy consciously the style of another, if you are trying to learn and have reached the age when you are capable of recognizing such a thing as style in swinging the club.

Learning to play golf as a youngster and learning after you have reached mature years are two different matters, for the very simple reason that the child still has the benefit of imitative instinct with which nature endows the young of all animals. But as the capacity to reason things out and to analyze actions begins to develop, the imitative instinct begins to fade. A child watches a performance and his mind registers a picture of the action as a whole. He will be unable to analyze it in detail and to describe its successive stages, but imitative instinct will enable him to make a creditable effort at reproducing the action as a whole after he has watched it a few times.

56

Along this line a rather interesting story went the
rounds some years back concerning Bobby Jones
and his first appearance in the United States
Amateur Championship, at the age of fourteen. A
well-known golf writer, watching him drive from a
tee some distance away, is said to have remarked
that he could almost believe that it was Stewart
Maiden hitting the ball. Maiden was the instructor
at the club in Atlanta where the youngster started
golf. Also Maiden was a boyhood chum in Scotland
of the golf writer, who was quite familiar with his
swing. I can't vouch for the truth of the story, but
it is a good one just the same. Incidentally, it is
told of Mr. Jones that as a small boy he was an
excellent mimic, and used to amuse friends of the
family with his imitations of the peculiarities of
different more or less eccentric players at the
club.

It is quite logical that youngsters, boys especially, since they are more likely to take readily to
the game, should come to pattern their efforts
on the performances of those who come under their
observation. It is the instinctive thing, because
of their imitative capacity. Furthermore, they will
naturally select the better players as models, and
players of this class swing. Imitative reproduction
therefore takes the form of swinging, and in time
the swinging action becomes habitual, quite without conscious effort to make it so, other than as the
imitative instinct directs.

However, as has been pointed out, such instinctive imitation is a different process entirely from a conscious attempt to copy this or that detail of the action by a person who has watched a swing and succeeded in picking up only a few high lights, so to speak, through attempting to analyze the action from observation. To appreciate the contrast, recall the remarkably easy rhythm you have observed when a caddie has sneaked a swing with one of your clubs, contrary to the caddie master's instruction, and then think back to the efforts you have seen in players to acquire a finishing pose with the club back over the left shoulder, after going through all kinds of contortions in swiping at the ball.

There is difficulty enough for most of us in learning how to swing by the simple process of coming to sense the action through feeling what is being done with the club head, without adding to the problem by trying to imitate the appearance of others at the same time. Your gait in walking may not be so elegant as that of others, but it gets results. We cannot all be fine stylists, but we can all develop form in doing a thing if we go about it in an intelligent way. Form refers here to a capacity to do a thing many times over in substantially the same way. Development of a swinging action is the surest and safest approach to acquiring dependable form in striking a golf ball.

VARIATIONS IN THE SWING

I SHOULD not be surprised to learn that some are disappointed at the failure, up to this point, to find any specific reference on how to use the different clubs in the bag, such, for instance, as "How to Drive," "How to Play the Mashie," and so on. I know that it is quite customary to go into detail on the discussion of the use of different clubs. So let us clear this matter up here and now. The golf stroke, in its basic essentials, is the same with all clubs.

From the driver or brassie right down to the putter, it is a swing. You may vary the swing, but you must not vary from it. I have already stated that I cannot say I have ever seen two players swing exactly alike. Yet there are thousands of good players, and all of them swing. No further

59

proof is needed of variations in the manner of swinging.

Moreover, all good golfers can and do vary their own swings at times to meet the peculiar requirements of the stroke to be played. If, for example, conditions of play require that the ball be made to rise abruptly on being struck, the player not only chooses a club with plenty of loft but he also executes a notably upright swing. Yet he *swings* the club head just the same. The plane in which it is swung changes naturally.

Playing from difficult lies likewise involves special problems in adapting the swing to meet the existing conditions. In dealing with an uphill or downhill lie, for example, the player must make due allowance for maintaining his sense of balance through the stroke. But this is no puzzling problem so long as he has acquired the knack of swinging so that it has become habitual. He has to do the same thing in walking uphill or downhill or along the side of a hill. But he gives no conscious thought to the adjustments necessary to these special conditions. His muscular actions respond to the central purpose of keeping the body balanced, without conscious effort to do so. So also in playing a golf stroke.

There is a popular belief that the stroke with iron clubs is more of a hit than with woods. It

60

may be conceded that, in watching even an expert player, one may sense more of what may be called "punch" with irons than is apparent in the fuller stroke with wood clubs. The reader will recall the distinction, between "hitting" and "swinging" made in an earlier chapter. Also I may repeat an earlier assertion that no one swings perfectly. There is always an impulse to use more power than we can apply properly, that is, by swinging. When we inject more power than we can control, we introduce a degree of leverage, but, when it creeps in near the end, that is, just before impact, it may produce no appreciable damage, provided the stroke has started as a swing and this action has been maintained almost up to the instant of impact.

Furthermore, whatever of leverage is introduced in the brief instant just preceding impact is restricted to pure hand and wrist action, and does not involve conflicting actions between body movement and arm movement, which are bound to follow the introduction of leverage in starting the stroke. That is to say, if a levering method of applying the power in wielding the club prevails in starting the stroke, the later cannot develop as a swing. On the other hand, if the action is a swing from its inception, the hands and arms will swing on through, maintaining the swinging character-

61

istic as the dominant movement, even though some small degree of leverage develops through the hands and wrists just before and at impact.

There is another ready explanation of the appearance of more "hitting" or "punch" in the stroke with irons, where the stroke is less than a full swing. For these shorter strokes, obviously the turning of the body both on the backward and on the forward swings is not so full as with a full-length swing. Yet the bending or flexing of the wrists is quite as full. For, if the player swings the club, the weight of the club head will pull the hands to where the wrists are fully bent, before the change in direction by the club head begins to take place.

Also it should be borne in mind that the wrists act as hinges, so to speak, joining the hands and arms, and that the natural outward pull of the club head will cause them to bend forward, as the speed of the club head is built up to a maximum at impact, in a real swinging action, quite independent of a conscious attempt to put "wrist snap" into the stroke. It is obvious, of course, that the action of the wrists at the stage where the club head is changing direction brings about a position of the hands, in their relation to the forearms, quite different from that in the address. It is equally obvious that the hands must come back to a like position in the address, so that the face of

Leo Diegel, *well-known professional, has scored in the low 70's for a round of 18 holes, playing each stroke, while standing on his right foot alone. This sequence of pictures shows him at varying stages in the swing, and is offered here as proof that balance during the*

swing is responsive to the main purpose of swinging the club head with
the hands. Diegel gives no thought to the details of how the body turns,
whether playing from one foot or two. Balance accompanies the action
in both cases, and is not consciously contrived.

the club shall be brought squarely against the ball. But this return to position can and will be brought about by a swinging action, without conscious effort on the player's part to put so-called "wrist snap" into the stroke.

On the other hand, conscious efforts on the part of the player to gain distance by striving to introduce wrist action almost invariably lead to trouble. For the expert player, it usually means a shot far off the intended line, more often than not to the left. In his effort to get extra distance, he introduces leverage through too powerful action with the right hand. Remember that, since the left hand is the one on the end of the club (I am speaking now, of course, of right-handed players), it must guide and direct the action. If the right is allowed to inject too much power, the extra power takes the form of levering.

For the high-handicap player, conscious efforts to introduce wrist action also result in levering. The chief reason for his being a high-handicap player is his failure to learn a swinging action with the club head in the first place, but the result he gets will probably differ from that of the more expert player in that his effort at "putting the wrists into it" finds the forward sweep of the hands practically stopped by the time the club head reaches the ball, except for a kind of forward flick of the wrists. This, I repeat, is what usually happens when the high-handicap player purposely tries to introduce wrist action consciously.

The foregoing paragraph does not mean to imply that the wrists do not perform an important function in swinging the club. They are vastly important. As I have explained, they make it possible to retain the easy smooth rhythm of a swinging action through the change in direction of the club head from the preliminary back sweep of the club head until it has been swung up and around at the finish of the swing. But their action, like that of other parts of the body, should be entirely responsive to the main purpose of causing the club head to move with a swinging action.

Thus, if it has appeared to you that the stroke with an iron club is more of a hit than that with a driver or brassie, be assured that the same guide to controlled speed in the full stroke, that is, a swing with the club head, is just as important with the irons. Be content with developing that sense of feel of what is happening with the club head for irons as well as for woods.

Of course, one varies the swing from long strokes to short ones, in the sense that the action is cut down. But again there is no variation in the character of the action; it is still a swing from the tee shot right down to the putt. Strangely enough, there appears to be more difficulty in maintaining the swing in the shorter strokes, until one has

64

PLAYING *a stroke from a sitting position, a demonstration used to show that no concern need be felt for whether the legs, hips, or other parts of the body will do their respective parts, so long as the player is conscious of swinging the club head with his hands. The actions of these members during the stroke are responsive, not initiative.*

thoroughly developed the idea of sensing a feel of the club head at all times, than in the longer ones. Even among very good players one usually finds more badly played short strokes than full ones.

A probable reason for this is that the longer action of the full strokes afford more time to acquire a feel of the club head. With the short ones there is a tendency to hurry the thing through and have it done with. Always a hurried stroke is more likely to be marked by leverage. And a hurried start has no place in a swing, which always begins slowly and smoothly.

In this connection, I want to say a word for the benefit of those who are inclined to feel that they must strike a certain kind of pose in order to bring about a stroke which they assume resembles that of some player they have seen. Invariably they assume a position for starting the swing, which is supposed to develop a certain position at the top of the backswing or at some other stage of the stroke. Needless to say, they are thinking in terms of body posture and not in terms of hand action.

One can swing a club from almost any position, if one understands what swinging means and knows how to identify it through feel. The reader has possibly at some time or other watched trick-shot performers hit the ball from different awkward stances and positions. I can sit in a chair and drive a ball 200 yards, and I frequently use this simple device to prove to pupils that, whereas there is one simple and comfortable way to stand to the ball, as has already been described, there are many ways that one may stand and still swing. The important thing is to learn to swing, and to know when you are swinging and when you are not. You will develop your own pattern of swinging just as you have developed that of walking, and you may vary it from time to time consciously, or even sub-consciously. In fact, you will be a rare exception if your are ever able to swing in exactly the same way day after day for any given length of time. But the ability to swing and to know a swinging action by feel is the only hope for permanent improvement in golf.

ACCURACY AND HOW IT IS ATTAINED

IN an earlier chapter I asserted that both greater
speed and greater accuracy in wielding the club
head can be attained, with a given amount of force,
through a swinging application than in any other
way. Considerable space has been devoted to the
factor of speed. Now I want to take up the matter
of accuracy in bringing the face of the club head
against the ball at the desired angle.

For purposes of comparison, consider the action
of a spinning top. It is the rotary motion in a
horizontal plane that causes the top to stand on
end, in defiance of the pull of gravity, so long as
that rotary force is strong enough to resist the pull,
which eventually causes the top to fall on its side.
The faster the top spins, the steadier the orbit in

which it turns. It is only when the spinning speed begins to slow down perceptibly that the top begins to wobble, and eventually falls.

The characteristics of a swing action are the same in all cases, no matter how the action is manifested. Hence the greater the speed developed in swinging the club head, the steadier and truer the orbit in which it is swung. But regardless of the speed, a swinging action is necessary to keep the club head moving in substantially the same path time after time. In other words, only the steady, smooth application of power exemplified in a true swing will enable the player to approach consistency in wielding the club with accuracy.

Only scant consideration is needed to convince one of the improbability that any player, with the hands placed at one end of a club and the club head at the other, from 36 to 40 inches apart, can consciously direct the forward movement of the club head so as to strike the ball with the accuracy needed to hit it along the intended line. A variation of 1 degree would mean something like 10 feet in 200 yards, and 3, 4, or 5 degrees would be a small margin of error in trying consciously to regulate the angle of striking. It should be plain, therefore, that there can be little hope for accuracy along this line.

Accuracy and control are not to be obtained in this manner in golf any more than a baseball pitcher acquires control in throwing the ball where he wants it to go by thinking of such details as the exact instant at which he releases his hold on it. The pitcher develops control by developing a muscular routine, through constant practice, until he reaches a stage where he instinctively releases his grip on the ball without any conscious thought whatever of that detail. Once he has attained this stage, he will, as a rule, be able to throw the ball accurately so long as he employs the speed that his muscular routine normally develops. But when he tries too hard to develop extra speed, he will probably find difficulty in maintaining control.

The situation is quite the same with the golfer. Once he has developed a muscular routine founded on swinging, he can go on time after time wielding the club with accuracy, and at the same time developing as high a speed as the power employed is capable of producing. But so long as he plays golf, so long will the impulse to apply more power than he can control seize him from time to time. He may exert a more powerful physical effort, but it is likely that the extra power will be misapplied. That is, it will not radiate from the center, as must always be the case in a real swing, but will be introduced in the form of leverage, through application at some other point.

When the baseball pitcher begins to have difficulty in controlling the pitch, he does not try to regain his control by tampering with his method of

69

holding the ball or by trying to throw harder. On the other hand, he attempts to get back to his normal movement in throwing. He knows full well that he has a better chance of bringing the pitch under control in this way than by any other. Once more the case is the same with the golfer.

The only safe and reliable way to get back to striking the ball squarely with the face of the club is to make sure of three things: first, see that the club is being held correctly; second, see that you are standing properly in relation to the ball to hit it where you are aiming; third, make a smooth free swing. If the player holds the club properly, stands in the correct position, and takes a normal swing, the ball must travel in the line selected, or very close to it. These are the three considerations that determine control of direction. Failure to obtain it in a shot can be traced back to the lack of one or more of them in playing the stroke.

I would like the reader to ponder the preceding paragraph carefully. It is very important, especially in consideration of the claim that "one must do more than swing the club head" to play good golf. This assertion, I take it, is prompted by observation of the difference in outward appearances of well-known players, and again is evidence that the observer is concerning himself with nonessentials and is missing entirely the basic fundamental— that all good players swing.

70

The point of confusion is that the observer watches certain detailed movements and actions, which he takes to be essential to the player's success. If he followed carefully any player of his choice, he would observe that these mannerisms are present with the player when he is playing below his best form, even as they are when he is playing especially well. But that point is likely to escape him. He also would, if he questioned his model, get the answer that, when the latter is playing well, he is playing very easily; furthermore that, when he begins to play badly, the harder he tries, the more difficult the game becomes.

Whether his model has analyzed his own game well enough to know it or not, it is smooth, easy stroking with a correct grip and stance, which produce for him satisfactory distance, and fine control of direction as well. It distinctly is not some pet device that he is trying out at the time, to enable him to produce consciously accurate control or greater distance, except as such a device prompts him to swing more smoothly and steadily.

It is quite easy to understand the deduction of those who study the playing of the game from the viewpoint of outward appearances, in arriving at the conclusion that certain mannerisms are of importance. It is equally easy to understand the derivation of differences in mannerisms. Reference now is to those who play well, of course. That they do play well is evidence that the stroke with them is basically a swing. How they came to attain it is immaterial. But each is an individual, and, if he has attained mature age, he has without doubt done no little experimenting. He has resorted to the old practice of trial and error until he has worked out something that he is convinced is best suited to his own needs.

Experiments of this kind may run through considerable range, in change of grip, stance, body adjustment before starting the swing, waggling, and so on, until the player eventually works out at least a temporary solution of his problem. Actually, the change may involve to a mild degree a physical handicap, but, if it happens to produce results temporarily, it may afford a real help on the mental or psychological side. The player sets his mind at ease in the conviction that his new discovery is going to solve a certain problem. This done, he is then much more likely to swing smoothly and steadily.

I know of a case of a well-known businessman, who consistently cuts seven or eight strokes off his score when playing with a certain noted professional by employing a very simple procedure. For each stroke, the professional takes his stance to play the stroke, marks his footprints distinctly, and then tells his companion to stand in those tracks and hit the ball. This man has been playing golf for years, and it would be utterly ridiculous to suppose that he does not know how to stand to the ball to play a stroke. But the simple trick of having the professional indicate the exact stance removes from the other man's mind all doubt as to whether he is standing properly, and helps him to concentrate on making the stroke.

I have mentioned this case for the simple purpose of showing how the mental aspect of the game affects the physical, a subject that will be taken up more fully in the following chapter, and also for the purpose of tying up with the discussion of accuracy through swinging the many various devices that are supposed to come under the heading of other things that one may be called on to do, besides swinging the club head. As stated above, it is not an uncommon thing to find players employing certain devices that actually make the game harder for them. I am referring now to good players. Faulty gripping, exaggerated types of stance, and so on are included in such a list.

Such players play well, and might play even better, and certainly more consistently, with sounder methods. Yet their scoring is such as to bring them to the attention of others who are trying to improve their play. They have acquired the basic fundamental of swinging, and many of their mannerisms, as stated above, may actually make swinging more difficult than it should be. Such physical handicaps in handling the club must in time take their toll. This fact accounts for the great amount of experimenting that goes on even among good players. Among so-called "duffers" this sort of thing is vastly multiplied. There are and have been numberless "tips" supposed to cure this fault or that. Naturally enough, some of them are entirely sound and consistent with correct stroking of the ball. But even these have the shortcoming of dealing only with some single phase of the stroke, whereas the latter is a unit action that cannot be taken apart and treated piece by piece. Other tips and suggestions are far worse because they are not even consistent with correct stroking.

But the worst feature of this approach to learning the game is the fact that it means going about the task backward from the very first. It is a matter of correcting that which is wrong, instead of learning that which is right. A tip to correct one fault may in time produce an equally damaging fault of itself. Furthermore, no matter how much of this sort of thing is done, the fact remains that any plan which supposes that the player is bringing about control in any way other than by smooth swinging from a sound base is doomed to failure.

One of the leading golf writers in this country once remarked: "Bobby Jones trusts his swing to a higher degree than any other golfer I have ever

seen. If he is off line on a shot, he may be off
30 yards. Some of the other stars appear to sense
that something is wrong, and to make at least a
partial correction in the hand action as the club
head is brought against the ball. But once Jones
starts his swing, he goes right through with it
without any attempt at correction."

This is nothing more than saying that Mr. Jones
was more intent on swinging the club head than
the others. And over a period of ten or eleven years
during which he played in open championships, it
may be recalled that he was far and away the most
consistent player of them all. This remarkable
consistency—in the eleven United States Open
Championships in which he took part he never
once scored as high as 80—is eloquent testimonial
to his success at achieving accuracy in striking the
ball through "trusting his swing," as compared
to the efforts of others who may have tried to introduce corrective measures through conscious manipulation in the course of making the stroke.

Such efforts to control the club by conscious
direction are usually referred to as "steering," and
the consequences are well known to all experienced
players. They are the result of conscious interference with the performance of an action which
normally is, and in all cases should be, subconsciously controlled. This is manifested in the results
obtained when one tries to play a stroke with

restraint quite as much as when one tries to overdo it. Both cases involve the same difficulty—conscious interference. The results emphasize the necessity of depending for accuracy as well as for speed of the club head on developing a swinging action, which is sensed and controlled through feeling in the hands what is being done with the club head.

THE MENTAL SIDE

ANY general discussion of golf and how to play
it well must take note of the mental side of
the game. One frequently hears it said that golf is
largely a mental problem, and in one respect that
is undoubtedly true. It all depends on what is to be
considered the "mental side" of the game. If reference is to the conscious thought required in
wielding the club, this is of little consequence. No
considerable amount of intelligence is needed to
swing a club.

On the other hand, if reference is to one's mental
activities in the course of playing a stroke, and the
complications these may introduce, the "mental
side" is indeed of very great importance, because
one's mental processes, conscious and subconscious,
direct one's physical actions, and it is a dominant

77

characteristic of the conscious processes that they
interfere with the subconscious processes. In golf
they affect high and low alike, because they interfere not only with the proper performance, after it
has been developed to a stage where it can be taken
care of subconsciously, but to the learning of the
performance in the first stages.

It should be apparent to any player, on brief
reflection, that he plays golf, if he plays it well,
largely through subconscious control, even as he
does a thousand other commonplace things every
day of his life. Through one process or another he
develops a muscular routine, which from constant
repetition becomes habitual, that is to say, subconsciously controlled. Once this has been accomplished, he goes along repeating the performance
whenever a situation demands it, without any
conscious consideration of the manner in which it
is done.

Consider, for example, the simple process of
signing one's name. The reader surely could write
his signature a thousand times, and each and every
specimen would be readily recognizable as being
essentially the same as every other. Moreover, he
could do so while sitting and chatting with an
acquaintance or otherwise employing his conscious
mental processes. But make the following simple
test: Write your signature as you ordinarily do.
Then, in the space beneath it, try consciously to

78

copy it, directing each successive move of the pen or pencil to produce each letter in exact likeness of the one above. Then compare the two, and consider the difference.

It may also be observed that the easier, smoother, and more flowing the natural action of the pen in the ordinary manner of writing, the more pronounced will be the difference. There is distinct

Efforts *during the swing to concern the conscious mind with any one of numberless details of the outward appearance of someone else must inevitably interfere with subconscious control of the swing. You should think only of sensing a feel of what you are doing with the club head through the action of the hands.*

79

rhythm in a free, easy style of writing; in fact, rhythm is highly essential to good penmanship. And rhythm, of course, is also essential to a proper stroking of the ball in golf. There is an exact parallel between the two performances as regards direction by subconscious control and direction by conscious control.

The urge, intentional or otherwise, to try to control the movement of the club head through consciously directed effort interferes with the golfer, whether he is a beginner or an expert. In the case of the latter, it explains his lapses from form from time to time. In the case of the former, it explains most of the troubles he has in learning to develop the routine of correct stroking, which is the foundation of any permanent improvement in his play.

In the case of the expert, it is said that he is unable to concentrate properly, which prompts me to remark that concentration is probably the most misunderstood term in golf. It does not mean actively thinking of any one detail of the stroke, but rather the opposite—refusal to allow any single detail to absorb the attention. Frequently, when a player thinks he is concentrating very hard on the stroke he is about to play, he is doing nothing more than worrying over one detail of the stroke, or possibly, what is even worse, over the probable outcome of the stroke; sometimes he is worrying to

80

THE BODY *turns in swinging, but a swing is not produced by centering attention on the turning. The two figures to the left show reverse body positions when swinging the club with the hands held wide apart; those on the right similar position in swinging the club in the normal way. The top figures show the turn accomplished as the player, with the club held in the arms across the back, seeks to point first one end of the club and then the other at the ball. The purpose is to point the club; the turn is a resulting movement.*

such an extent that he permits his muscular system to tighten up to a point where it is a physical impossibility for him to effect a real swing.

However, the purpose here is to serve first those who are still laboring with the problem of laying the foundation for a consistently good game, that is, those who have as yet to learn how to swing and how to know when they are swinging. So it is the main job to get ahead with the discussion of the mental problems that beset them in this important task of learning to swing.

Too much imagination is a serious stumbling block to most persons in learning to play golf. Imagination is an active function of conscious thinking. It is one of the most important factors in the lives of all of us. We begin exercising it in childhood, and go right along through life indulging it every day. Yet, when it comes to learning to play golf, what a wonderful thing it would be to be able to turn off the imagination just as we do at a faucet. That, of course, is quite impossible, for the imagination will continue to function during our waking hours, whether we wish it or not, and the field of golf is no exception in its range of activities.

I have given lessons to thousands of golfers, and nine out of ten of them were quite willing in the beginning to tell me what was wrong with their games. Actually, of course, if they had known, they should not have felt any need to come to me, or to go to anyone else for instruction. But they overlook this inconsistency in the enthusiasm of their theorizing about the game. Within a short time after a person has taken up golf, almost from the beginning, he begins to form certain conceptions of the stroke and how it is made. Invariably these conceptions take form from what he has been able to gain through the sense of visual observation. On the basis of these observations, his imagination goes to work in formulating different theories.

You may recall from the Foreword a quotation from Sir Walter Simpson, written fifty years ago, on this matter of theorizing. As he pointed out, we have to stand for theorizing on the player's part as a concession to him as a thinking animal. But he must recognize it as a recreation and understand that it may easily prove one of the most serious obstacles to his progress in learning to play well.

Already I have called attention to the necessity of learning the game through the sense of touch or feeling, not through the sense of sight. This fundamental fact explains a great many of the golfer's difficulties, which arise from his theorizing. He is making the serious mistake of trying to reproduce certain physical actions that he has seen in others. It is beside the point that these actions are entirely orthodox and consistent with fine stroking. The matter of chief concern is to develop the

82

method of stroking, and the model himself never developed his method in that way.

Let me illustrate how easily such a mistake can interfere with the orderly and positive way of learning through cultivating a sense of feel of the correct action. A short time ago, I had a pupil who had been making very satisfactory progress through several lessons. In the course of talking things over one day, I emphasized the necessity of starting everything together in beginning the swing, as contrasted with making this or that movement the initial one. In explaining this point further, I remarked that the hands must swing the club back, and that it must not be pushed, pulled, or hauled. While I was demonstrating just what I meant, the pupil noticed that my hands appeared to start slightly before the club head was moved.

Nothing was said of this matter at the time, but the action made an impression on his mind, and, in the light of what I had said, he concluded that this was wrong and something to be avoided. When he came back a few days later for another lesson, I noticed right away that something had halted his progress. Tenseness and stiffness were readily evident in each of his attempts to swing the club. I asked him what had caused him to tighten up, and he then told me what he had observed about the movement of the hands during the demonstration in the previous lesson. He had been watching his hands during practice swinging in the meantime and had been trying to keep them from moving as mine had.

Now, as a matter of fact, that particular action of itself was of no consequence whatever. There are many fine golfers who appear to "drag" the club head back from the ball. It is quite possible that some of them may have adopted the practice by design, because they were convinced that it served a certain purpose, such, for instance, as insuring freedom and flexibility in the wrists, or guarding against holding the club too tightly. But here again we are considering nothing more than a mannerism, and neither this nor any other such small device ever made anyone a good golfer. Undoubtedly such a player had already learned the knack of swinging, and this "drag" was incidental. More than likely, should it occur to the player that he might achieve better results by starting hands and club head together, he could, with but little practice, entirely eliminate this little business.

Yet even so small a thing as that proved a definite interruption to that particular pupil. He could not restrain his imagination from attaching importance to the relation of what I had said to him about pushing, pulling, or hauling the club back to the fact that he observed my hands describe a certain movement while I was demonstrating faulty ways of starting. The imagination is constantly operating with information and intelligence communicated to the mind, and it so happens that the sense of sight is the most important of all the senses in gathering such information and intelligence. His sense of sight could detect the physical appearance of the action, whereas his sense of touch could not, of course, register the feel that I, who was wielding the club, experienced.

Then again, I find that most persons appear to retain certain mental reservations in the face of any statement of fact made to them, without necessarily implying any distrust of the source of the statement or of the actual authenticity of the facts. All of us incline toward the feeling that somehow or other we are the exceptions to the general rule.

I fully appreciate the possibility that the reader, at this very instant, is experiencing reservations to statements set forth here and earlier in these pages. Possibly he questions the fact that greater speed and greater accuracy in striking the ball can be developed, with any given amount of power, through swinging than otherwise. He may not be entirely convinced that a more dependable routine of stroking can be developed by learning to sense a swinging action with the club head than by any other process. Well, I have conceded that it is possible for persons to learn to play golf through a process of visual analysis of the stroke, as made by others, through its varying phases, in time piecing

these several detailed movements together, but
I insist that this is the difficult way. In support of
my claim, I can point to countless thousands who
have been trying to do this for many years with no
appreciable success.

I have touched on these matters, bearing on the
difficulties that the imagination or conscious
mental processes may and do introduce into the
problem of learning to play golf. Much more might
be said as to how the mental state affects the
player during the playing of a stroke. In the discussion of Obstacles to Swinging, reference was
made to how the mental attitude of the player can
and does prompt him to try to inject more power
than he can control, and, by so doing, causes endless
difficulties through converting the application of
power from a swing to levering. There are addi-
tional difficulties arising from the player's concern
over the probable outcome of the shot at hand.

He may, for example, be concerned with danger
from a near-by boundary line, which may take its
toll of a crooked shot, or a hazard to be carried, or
the selection of the proper club, and so on. All these
come, of course, under the heading, the mental
side. They are all to be treated with the same
prescription. Learn to settle the issue in advance of
the start of the stroke, and, once that has been
started, concentrate only on the idea of feeling the
swinging action of the club head.

Obviously we cannot will the mind to remain absolutely blank. It must concern itself with something, and there may be a thousand things more or less that will engage its attention, unless we can discipline it to concern itself with some one definite thing. Aim at making that one thing consciousness of a feel of swinging the club head. Try to think of that and nothing else.

In this connection, I may recall to the reader's attention what has been said about the sense of sight, and the importance it has in conveying impressions to the mind. Just as it reveals more than any of the other senses, so it is the medium of introducing more interferences and distractions, when one tries to concentrate on any one thought. Therefore, in practicing to learn to sense a feel of swinging the club head, it is helpful to close the eyes while swinging. You will note at once that the sense of touch or feel functions more readily when the sense of sight has been shut off. This suggestion has proved very helpful with a great many of my pupils in actual teaching.

PROFIT FROM PRACTICE

IN a sense, what has gone before has been presented with a twofold purpose. First, I have tried to point out that one must accept the golf stroke as a swinging action of the club head, in its basic essential, in order to make any permanent headway in learning to play the game consistently well. The second phase has been an outlining of ways and means of developing a swinging action in wielding the club, through learning to know it and to identify it by the feel as experienced in the hands.

Once this has been done, the player is on the high road to a reasonable degree of skill, with a definite positive guide always at hand, to which he may turn in times of need. He is also on the way to a fuller enjoyment of the game than he has previously known. But this does not mean to say that he has mastered it. For no man has ever become a perfect swinger. By that I mean to say that no one ever has been, or ever will be, able to make a perfect swing at will. He may make ten, twenty, thirty, or more successive strokes with approximate perfection, and yet never have positive assurance that the next will be as good.

Only a machine can perform a mechanical action perfectly, and a machine has no brain, no imagination, no mental kinks to interfere with its performance. On the other hand, the machine never can, of course, experience the satisfaction that comes from a successful performance, the accomplishment of an objective. I know of few more satisfying experiences than the thrill that comes from conquering the many obstacles involved in developing real skill in playing golf, by one who has known the hard work and worry and anguish that can result from playing it badly.

Within reasonable limitations, the degree of skill that one may reasonably expect to develop, once he has learned the art of swinging, will depend largely on intelligent application of the principle he has learned through practice. It is by frequent repetition that any action becomes habitual, that is, subconsciously controlled. The great Paderewski is said to have remarked once, "If I miss one day of practice, I can tell it in my playing; if I miss

two days in succession, my audience can tell it."
I would not go so far as to say that the technique
of swinging a golf club is so finely tempered as that,
but practice and skillful play are very intimately
associated.

Intelligent practice will confirm the player in the
performance of the swing and will continually
increase the probability that each stroke will
approach closer to perfection in performance.
What is of even greater importance is constant and
continued training in keeping concentration cen-
tered on that feeling of the swinging action of the
club head. The muscular routine can in time be
developed to the point where there will be little
likelihood of variation, when it functions free of
conscious interference. But there can never be any
letup on the effort to keep the conscious mind
riveted on sensing the feel of the swing.

Reference has already been made to the fact that
expert players differ from one another in certain
outward appearances. It has likewise been stated
that the differences are largely individual mannerisms, which are more or less incidental. In many
cases they are the results of an intentional striving
for a certain effect; in others they have been
developed quite unintentionally. In all cases they
serve chiefly to distinguish the individual, even as
persons differ one from another in the way they
walk.

90

These differences, however, lead to a consideration of the style and form of different players, or rather to a discussion of these two terms as they relate to golf, since they are widely misunderstood. "I cannot understand," says one, "how it is that Blink plays such a wretched game; he has such a fine style"; or "I don't see how Blank manages to hit the ball at all with that terrible form that he has."

Our hypothetical commentators are merely confused, of course, in their understanding of the two terms. "Form," the dictionary tells us, "is established method of expression or practice." Style is defined as "mode or manner which is deemed elegant, or in accord with a standard; a distinctive or characteristic manner or method.'

In other words, form is the capacity for doing a thing in substantially the same way over and over again. If the manner is easy, graceful, and free from the appearance of undue effort, it is good form. Good form appeals to the eye and is style. Style, or the lack of it, so far as golf is concerned, is that which the eye perceives in the performance of others. Form is the player's manner of producing the performance. If, true to the definition, the method of expression or practice is established, it is directed by the sense of feel, and not by sight. Form, however awkward, will produce relatively consistent results. Style of performance has no relation to results, except as it indicates good form.

I have introduced this comment here to emphasize once more the folly of trying to copy the mannerisms or styles of other players. It is form alone that counts in building up consistency of performances. Obviously enough, the sounder the form, the more consistent the results obtained. But in any event, efforts to imitate what you see in the bodily actions of another in playing a golf stroke cannot possibly prove of any help to you in discovering the feel of the action that the player himself experiences.

This prompts me to comment briefly on what may profitably be derived from watching expert players in action, and what to look for as they play the stroke. Usually when I am giving a lesson I carry with me a small booklet showing successive stages of the stroke by Bobby Jones. It is arranged in sequence from front to back, and, by flipping the pages between the thumb and forefinger, I can produce the effect of an actual motion picture of the stroke. In calling it to the attention of my pupils, I ask them to watch only the movement of the club head and to disregard the body actions. Almost without fail, pupils immediately perceive that the club head moves almost as though it were a weight on a string. In other words, within practical limits, the movement is a near-perfect swinging action from first to last.

Therein lies the value in watching the experts in actual play. Observe the steady rhythmic movement of the club head, or note the action of the hands in their movement through the stroke. In other words, try to register a picture of the action as a whole, and avoid efforts to pick out single details of this or that position at varying stages of the stroke. The hands hold and control the club. Their movement is directed by the central idea of swinging the club head, and succeeding movements of the body, legs, and other parts of the anatomy must be responsive to that one idea.

It should not be necessary to point out that practice, to be of any value whatsoever, must be carried out along sound lines. The mere act of going through the motion accomplishes nothing, unless the player is able to assure himself that the stroke embodies a swinging action. If one has any doubt on this point, the very best thing to do is to get back to the beginning. Try making a short stroke, which requires little turning of the body, and keep at it until you are sure of the feel of the club-head movement. Then gradually increase the scope of the action. If necessary, go all the way back to swinging a weight on a string through a short arc, as was recommended in an early chapter on how to know and to recognize the swing.

Once you have positively identified the feel of a swing, you will be able to recognize it thereafter, but this does not mean that you will be able to

93

swing smoothly each time you go out to play or take up a club for practice. It may be that after a considerable layoff from play you will find difficulty at first when you try it again. On the other hand, the lapse of a few weeks or so between games may find you returning easily to the routine, when you do play again.

Illustrative of the above point, Miss Virginia Van Wie told me two years ago of an interesting experience she had undergone. Following her winning of the United States Championship at the Whitemarsh Valley Country Club early in October, she played no golf until the following January. During the fall months she did, however, play quite a bit of tennis, requiring quick sharp applications of leverage in the stroke. On her return to golf, her first round was a 95. The following day she began to get back into the routine of swinging, and scored an 86. In her third round, the day after that, she had a 79, marking an improvement of almost a stroke a hole over her first return after the long layoff. I may add that her single purpose in any and all practice sessions is to school her concentration on thinking only of the feeling of the club-head action.

If this simple plan is sufficient for her, winner of numerous championships, the fact should commend it to the careful consideration of less skillful players.

94

"SWING" TELLS THE STORY

MY message from the beginning has been a simple one: "Swing the club head." And the reader may recall the warning, sounded in the Foreword, of much repetition. That warning was prompted by the experiences of more than twenty years of practical teaching, and to this day I still find it necessary to go over and over that simple message. Its very simplicity seems to offer the most baffling problem. To some, golf just cannot be that simple. And yet it is. But I have not dared to hope that a presentation of the idea in written form would achieve results more favorable than personal verbal instruction.

There is certainly nothing revolutionary or radical in the idea, but it is something of a variation from the common procedure of teaching the game.

95

As a concession to those who are thoroughly familiar with the usual process of analyzing the stroke piece by piece, in this concluding chapter I propose to show how sound analysis on the above basis is entirely consistent with what has been said of the conception of the stroke as a swinging action.

To do this I have collected quotations from the writings of a number of the notable experts, who have sought to analyze the game for the benefit of others. These I am reproducing here, along with a brief comment on each, pointing out how the theories expressed coincide fully with the swinging idea.

ROBERT T. JONES, JR.: "The more I play and study golf, the more firmly do I become convinced that the only possibility of a 'grooved' swing lies in the dominant use of the left arm and side. I offer the following six suggestions for developing such a swing.

"1. At the start of the backswing, be certain not to lift the club with the right hand; start it back by a push with the left.

"2. Be sure that the hips and shoulders turn freely during the backswing. Do not leave the left heel on the ground.

"3. Keep the left arm extended and do not hug the right elbow in too tightly; allow the right side to be perfectly relaxed as the club is swung back.

96

"4. Be sure to cock the left wrist at the top of the backswing but hold the club firmly with the left hand, so that it is kept under control.

"5. Hit through with the left arm, and do not discharge the wrist cock too early in the downswing.

"6. Don't be afraid to hit the ball."

Considering the points made in their turn, I have pointed out that the hand on the end of the club must control and guide the action in swinging, even as he points out in his first paragraph, speaking, of course, in terms of the right-handed swinger.

1. Because of its position on the shaft, between the left, which must control, and the head of the club, the right hand must set up a levering process, if it is allowed to set the club head in motion. A stroke started in this way cannot develop a swinging action.

2. Any stroke sufficiently long to require that the club head depart from the line running through the objective and the ball makes it necessary for the body to turn to some extent. How much turn takes place is determined by the length of the stroke. For a full stroke, the maximum turn of the body consistent with freedom and comfort will take place, in response to the action of the hands in swinging the club head.

3. For practical purposes, the left arm and the shaft of the club are of a piece, establishing the radius of the swing. The expanding action of a

97

swing draws the medium through which the force is being transmitted taut at all times. In golf the left arm (with right-handed players) is an important section of that medium, and the pull of the swing extends it. Unless the right hand is allowed to interfere by introducing leverage, the right arm will fall naturally and comfortably down by the side as the club is swung back.

4. Flexibility in the wrists permits of the change in direction of the club head during the swing. The swinging action, starting slowly and smoothly, is still developing speed at a comparatively slow measure as this change of direction takes place. The increasing speed as the club head is swung down to the ball, with an ever-increasing pull by the club head at this stage, causes the wrists to react from the bending, which took place in the change of direction, and to contribute to developing maximum speed at impact.

5. The swinging action will cause the left arm to remain extended until after impact. The only way in which the action of the wrist in natural response to a real swing can be hurried is through an effort to inject power into the stroke with the right hand, immediately after the club has changed direction. This, as has been pointed out, means destroying the swing by means of leverage, that is, trying to apply the power at some point other than the center.

Action *snapshots of Bobby Jones, whose stroke reveals a beautiful rhythmic swinging movement of the*

club head throughout. Note in the lower picture the expanding outward pull of the club head, resulting from the swinging force.

6. A swing will develop the maximum speed possible with the club head from the power that can be properly applied. Efforts to hold back in the application or to turn on more than can be controlled by swinging will interfere with swinging.

JAMES BRAID: "Generally speaking, iron shots, particularly those played with the shorter irons, are played too quickly, and there is too much hurry at the turning part in the stroke."

Full explanation was made in an early chapter of how a flexing of the wrists makes possible the change in direction of the club head, and at the same time retains in the stroke the quality of a swing, from the start until after the ball has been struck. One cannot hurry a swing; the speed of the object being swung can be gradually increased, but not hurried. The actions criticized by Braid are foreign to swinging.

GEORGE DUNCAN: "In nearly every case of slicing, the trouble boils down to just this—lack of pivoting."

For anything like a full stroke, it is quite necessary that the body shall turn naturally to allow the hands to swing the club head back and upward. This turning will be quite responsive to the hand action, if the stroke is begun as a swing. If the stroke is begun through a levering process, the counter actions of certain sets of muscles against certain others will result in the failure of the body

99

to turn as it should. If the player makes sure of swinging, he need not concern himself in the least about causing the body to turn; that detail will take care of itself.

GRANTLAND RICE: "It is the locked body, the tightened body, the lunging body, that does most of the damage in preventing the hands and arms from swinging the club head."

The aforementioned conditions in the body result in most cases from a tense condition in starting the swing, due to faulty methods of holding the club, or from a wrong conception of what the player is trying to do, namely, hit the ball with all his might instead of swinging the club head, or from conflicting forces in starting the stroke. Swinging demands an easy, relaxed mental and physical condition to begin with. Conditions described in the preceding paragraph cannot develop through swinging.

SIR ERNEST HOLDERNESS: "The fault committed by many golfers is to keep the right knee stiff in starting the club down and on through the stroke, instead of letting it go through with the club head."

Even as the left side relaxes in order to permit the body to make an easy turn toward the right in the backward sweep, if the player swings, so the right leg and side relax in the downward and forward sweep, to permit the body to turn easily

ANOTHER *lady champion in action: Lady Heathcote Amory, formerly Miss Joyce Wethered. Here again control of the club head*

through the hands produces a swinging action, with a resultant pull by the club head, as contrasted with the use of leverage, which produces a contracting effect.

toward the left. No player who does not introduce leverage into the stroke from the very start, by pulling back with his right hand, will ever experience the trouble of finding his right leg stiff and straight at the knee as the club head sweeps down to the ball.

Miss Joyce Wethered: "Jerky and uncontrolled movements in which the position of the club head is felt to be lost are never included in a fine swing."

The term "swing" has been used here as synonymous with stroke, or movement of the club. A true swinging action can never be jerky, and, as Miss Wethered points out, a feel of where the club head is and what is being done with it is present throughout a swing.

Jerome D. Travers: "Let the arms pull the body through instead of the body pushing the arms through. This latter is the worst thing in timing."

There is always an outward pull of the club head when it is being moved by swinging. What is referred to above as "the body pushing the arms through" means nothing more than that the player is trying to apply power in the wrong way, just as though he tried to increase the speed of a weight being swung on the end of a string by pushing on the string at some intermediate point between the hand and the weight. The futility of such a procedure should be readily evident.

101

HORACE HUTCHINSON: "The right shoulder
down and loose, as the club is swung down from the
top of the swing, is the first great secret for striking
the ball as it should be struck."

So long as the movement retains the nature of a
true swing, the left arm will be the guiding agency
(for right-handed players) up to the stage of striking the ball. When this condition obtains, it is
quite natural that the right arm and side are
comparatively inactive over something like two-
thirds of the arc that the hands describe in moving
down from their position at the top to that at
impact. If the right hand is allowed to inject
leverage in starting the downswing, the right
shoulder action commended in the preceding
paragraph cannot develop.

WANDA MORGAN: "While I am quite sure that
one cannot get length without hitting hard, I am
equally sure that hard hitting alone will not
produce length."

The distinction here is, of course, the difference
explained under Obstacles to Swinging between
developing speed to strike the ball hard by swinging
and exerting effort to "hit" hard with an application of the power through leverage rather than
swinging. One may swing as hard as he can
swing.

GRANTLAND RICE: "You have to time a hit
perfectly, whereas a swing will time itself."

A smooth gradual application of power, producing gradual acceleration of club-head speed is a distinguishing characteristic of swinging. It is extremely difficult to control the application of power through leverage. Leverage is marked by tenseness, and tenseness defies control.

GENE SARAZEN: "One of the chief essentials of a long straight drive is a brace-up of the left side just before impact."

In a swing the body, turning to the right on the backswing to accommodate the sweep of the arms and hands in carrying the club back and up, finds itself supported chiefly by the right leg at the top of the backswing. Naturally enough, therefore, when moving in the reverse direction during the downswing, the left leg offers the support. The fact that this leg straightens and stiffens just before and during the time the ball is being struck, is merely evidence that the stroke has maintained its swinging action. Any slackening or collapse of the left leg at impact shows that the turning of the body toward the left, in compensation for the necessary turn toward the right in the backswing, has not taken place; therefore, the stroke was not a swing.

HARRY VARDON: "The upstroke is everything. If it is bad, the downstroke will be wrong, and the ball will not be properly driven."

This is entirely consistent, of course, with the premise that I have set up from the start—that

103

the stroke is a continuous action from start to finish. If it is begun in any manner other than as a swinging action, there is little chance that it will develop into a swing in its later stages. Leverage, employed in starting the action, will prevail throughout.

ROBERT T. JONES, JR.: "One essential element of the golf stroke, regardless of what path it may take, is a smooth, even acceleration from the top of the swing down to and through the ball."

Throughout these pages I have tried to point out that the only way to obtain a smooth, even acceleration of the speed of the club head is through a swinging action.

The foregoing are, I feel, sufficient to point out that intelligent observation and comment on correct methods of wielding the club, viewed from the standpoint of the outward appearances of good players in action, is entirely consistent with the conception of the stroke as a swinging action. As a definite and positive thing that can be identified through feel, swinging therefore offers, to any one who is willing to apply himself to learning it, an open approach to learning to play golf reasonably well.

Since the foregoing is true, I am convinced that it is the simplest and easiest way to learn the game, whether one is just taking it up or has been struggling unsuccessfully with it over a period of

ACTION PICTURES *of two fine lady golfers. Top and bottom, Miss Virginia Van Wie, former United States Champion, at the finish of the stroke and at the limit of the backswing. Both pictures suggest body movement quite free from restraint, in response to swinging the club head. Center, Miss Charlotte Glutting photographed just at impact, showing the arms fully extended, as a result of the outward pull by the club head exerted through the action of swinging.*

years. It is for this reason that the reader finds no reference here on how to correct the vast assortment of troubles manifested in efforts to wield the club otherwise than by swinging. Learn to swing, and you have found the high road to good golf.

There remains, however, just one further consideration, involving one bit of advice that is impressed on every golfer—Keep Your Eye on the Ball. To be sure, you look at the ball. If you are trying to strike something with any kind of tool or implement, naturally you look at it. The mere fact that you do look at it will not insure that you strike it as you intend. Doubtless the reader has had experiences in driving a nail or tack with a hammer which qualify him to give testimony to this fact. But looking at it helps just the same.

But remember this. No more conscious effort to look at the ball is needed in striking a golf ball than in driving a nail. We look at the nail as a matter of course, and we continue to look at it if we experience no impulse to turn the gaze elsewhere. It will be just as easy to look at the golf ball while we are striking it, if we can keep our attention from wandering. The surest way to prevent a distraction is to direct conscious attention to sensing a feel of the action of the club head.

On the other hand, if we consider looking at the ball as a definite thing that we are required to do, this fact in itself will tend to distract the attention from sensing that feel of the club-head action. I have seen players so intent on making sure that they "kept the eye on the ball" during a stroke that they completely lost sight of the important matter of striking the ball. Look at the ball, but do not make a ceremony of it. Almost any good player can hit the ball as far and as straight with his eyes shut as he can with them open, once he has taken up his position and addressed the ball. Like other attendant actions, the practice of looking at the ball will become entirely responsive, once the player has developed the routine of making a smooth, rhythmic swing.

In conclusion, let me remark once more that good golf is easy—easy to play and enjoyable. As Bobby Jones has remarked, "Correct use of the muscles of the body contributes great power, and easily controlled power, too. Incorrect use of them is entirely hopeless." Swinging is the easiest and simplest method of applying controlled power. Swing the club head!

Part II

GENERAL OBSERVATIONS WITH COMPARISONS OF THE JONES SYSTEM TO OTHER METHODS

By INNIS BROWN

A MATTER OF JOINT
RESPONSIBILITY

A FRIEND of mine insists that you cannot teach people to play golf, that is, good golf. Either they can and do play well, or they can't and don't. And he has been around mixing in the fray or looking on from the side-lines for twenty years or more. The records disprove his claim, of course, but his viewpoint is interesting because it represents conclusions drawn from extensive observations. He has seen more than a few earnest duffers awkwardly plugging away at what they believe to be the precepts given them by some professional instructor. His conclusion, thus arrived at, is not altogether illogical.

On the other hand, such a conclusion handles rather ruthlessly a revered old adage, "Where

109

there is a will, there is a way," and few will question
the will of those who have been infected with the
golf virus. It is an eloquent testimonial to the
appeal of the game that so many who take it up go
along year after year, playing badly or indifferently
at best. I know of no other athletic game of which
this is true to such an extent as in golf.

There can be little question of the will; the
difficulty lies in finding the way. And here the
responsibility for failure rests alike on pupil and
teacher. They are jointly liable: the one because
of the attitude he assumes when he takes up the
game, and the other for the lack of an understanding, positive manner of teaching.

Hitting a golf ball far and straight looks ridicu-
lously easy, when an expert at the game is doing the
hitting. It appears to the inexperienced onlooker
that he too could hit it far and straight if given a
chance. You just stand there and sock it, he muses;
there's nothing to it. If you take the time to follow
this idea into its detailed analysis, you are likely
to discover that herein lies the main source of
trouble with a very large percentage of the country's legion of high-handicap players.

This is one part of the responsibility that lies
with the player. An equally important part is an
expectancy to make short work of learning the
game, once it has begun. This is reasonable in the
beginning considering the false impression gathered

110

from first acquaintance. Yet the game has a way of disillusioning people rather brutally. Even players of many years' experience tend to feed on the hope that some time, somewhere, they are going to happen on the real secret to the game or find some short cut overnight, which will lop ten or a dozen strokes from their scores. They are continually looking for a prize package.

Of course, they are doomed to disappointment. There is no secret to good golf, any more than there is a secret to playing tennis well or to becoming an expert in almost any line of physical endeavor. Reasonably good form and long hard application are the answer. There is no reason why a player should not expect reasonable improvement right along, if he has been fortunate enough to start right. If he has started wrong, his best bet is to go back and start over again, learning the right way.

Here pupil and teacher meet on a common ground to contribute to the former's difficulties in learning to play well. If the pupil has had the misfortune to make a bad start, he need not expect to attain success from a patchwork job of piling one temporary cure on another, as different disappointing results beset him. If he encounters a professional teacher who undertakes to set him right by methods of this kind, he is simply riding for a greater fall.

I have talked with professionals who have explained that all they ever did was to try to give a pupil a temporary correction—a kind of local application, so to speak—because they pointed out that golfers as a rule expect too much. They are looking for someone who can make them good golfers in short order, in spite of perhaps years of struggling along with faulty methods of wielding the club. They are impatient at the thought of going back to fundamental principles, and they balk at taking the time to practice a new method until it begins to show real results.

Then again, I have encountered professionals who, beyond showing the player how to stand and how to hold the club, were able to do very little more in actually diagnosing the player's troubles. They were able to show him just how it was done, by swinging the club themselves. And they were also able to tell him that he was swaying, that he failed to keep his left arm straight, that he looked up too soon, or that he didn't follow through, and dozens of other things. But they were unable to go to the root of the matter, get hold of what was causing the player to display this or that fault, and, by so doing, suggest some particular bit of advice that would bring about a correction.

It seems evident, therefore, that, if a player is to make any worth-while permanent improvement in his golf game, he must realize that the game is easy to play when one knows how, but may be quite difficult for him to learn. Furthermore he must understand that a good golf game, like most other things that people esteem, must be bought at a price—in this case the price of an intelligent plan of learning, and enough patient practice to allow the plan to work. He must also satisfy himself that he is receiving his instructions from one qualified to teach him. Just how is he to satisfy himself on this point?

There are various methods of teaching. The reader, presumably, has read in the first part of this book Ernest Jones's detailed explanation of his method of teaching, why he first came to adopt it, and why he has gone on using it for some twenty years. He has been remarkably successful. He is basing his claims on what he has proved by practical application. There are many other good golf teachers, and teaching methods among them vary. But this one thing can be put down as positive and definite, admitting of no exceptions. Any method of teaching that does not proceed on recognition of a swinging action of the club head as the dominant movement of the stroke is misleading and contrary to basic fact.

Long and weary discussions have been held, for example, on the point of whether the right hand or the left hand does more work in hitting the ball. If we consider this question from the angle of what the two hands do or should do, we may help to clear this point up.

Without any doubt whatsoever, most expert players have a distinct feel of using the right hand to help put extra punch into the stroke a scant fraction of a second before the ball is hit. In fact, in the 1936 Open Championship at Baltusrol, a leading contender, after the first round, remarked to a group of four or five persons, "That fellow," extending his right hand, "cost me at least six strokes today." He had been badly plagued by "hooking." At the same time, it was undeniably true that the right hand had been very important in lashing out the long drives for which he is famous.

And yet, in their proper function, the right hand and arm are practically inactive in the stroke, from the start until the hands move down on the downswing to a position practically level with the hips. In the meantime, it is the left hand and arm that have established the radius of the swing, and have guided and directed the movement of the club all the way through the stroke until the hands get down to the approximate level of the hips. Furthermore the left hand and arm must continue to swing right on through until the ball has been struck.

You have been advised to follow through. I have. Twenty years ago I was told that all my trouble was due to a failure to follow through. That was quite the same as telling a man to avoid

114

banana peelings on the street after he has slipped on one and fallen. He knows the consequences, and so did I. But what we both needed was advice on how to avoid a recurrence.

My difficulty was very simple indeed. I was hauling the club back with the right hand, and trying to do practically the entire job of striking the ball with it, starting from the top of the downswing. So long as I continued to do so, there was no earthly chance for me to follow through. I was hitting at the ball, not swinging the club head. If the stroke is a swing up to the instant of impact, the player cannot keep from following through.

Again you may hear a discussion on which hand is used to start the club back in beginning the stroke. They are both used, as a matter of fact, working together as one. But the main consideration is not which hand plays the most important part, but whether the two are working in a manner to accomplish a necessary coordination between the movement of the hands and the movement of the rest of the body. Some fine players appear to start by dragging the club head away from the ball with the hands moving in a manner to cause the back of the left one to bend backward toward the left forearm; some appear to "sling" the club back; some claim to have a distinct feeling that the right hand is in control, though these are a very scant minority. But without a single exception, whatever their sensation in the starting stage, they get the leg and body coordination with the movement of the hands, necessary to let the hands get to the top of the swing, while working essentially as a unit.

All that has been said in urging that one be sure to see that the left hand and arm make the initial move of the club head is like the building of a guard rail on the ravine of a mountain road—no one ever falls off the road on the other side. Likewise, in every case where the player departs from the practice of making the two hands work as a unit in taking the club back, the error will be on the side of too active application of the right hand and arm.

Too much right hand results from a perfectly normal impulse. A right-handed player is right-hand conscious. He writes his name with his right hand and tips his hat with his right hand; when he goes fishing, he holds the rod in his right hand. The same is true in numberless other cases. It is entirely to be expected, therefore, that he should subconsciously seek to employ the right to do most of the work when he uses a golf club. And he does so until he is broken of the habit. Until he is broken of the habit, there is little or no chance that he is going to develop a swing with the club head. And until he does the latter, he is never going to be more than a mediocre golfer, easy prey to about every kind of fault to which golfing flesh can fall heir.

All these discussions and many more are the grist of the mill of golf debate, but you can judge of the worth of any contention on the premise set forth above. Does the theory coincide with what takes place in a real swinging action? If it does not, pass it up. Experienced, capable instructors use different methods and devices to encourage the player to develop a correct stroke. They may not at times talk in terms of a swing as such; one here and there may not even be aware of the physical distinction between swinging and leverage. But they will recognize the swinging quality in the player's stroke, when he is able to produce it. Their success as teachers will depend on the ease with which they are able to cause him to produce it.

So steel yourself to accept the dictum that no teacher can make you a good golfer. It is a partnership undertaking, and you have quite as much responsibility as he. Also accept the fact that you will have to work to succeed; "work" means that you will have to apply patiently the method given you. This is not a lot to exact, if you happen to be one of the many thousands who have actually labored for some years in an effort to get the hang of the game without any appreciable success.

Such "work" directed along the right line will prove a satisfaction and a pleasure, when you have

117

a definite and positive aim. Even a rough road is not so bad if you know where it is leading, and realize that satisfaction and enjoyment lie at the end. But aimless wandering must lead to monotony and discouragement, and extra zeal and ambition do not help the cause.

ADDING TO THE CONFUSION

WHATEVER routine an instructor may adopt in helping a pupil to improve his game, it is essential that both take into consideration two vitally important factors. First, so far as the physical action of wielding the club is concerned, golf is played through a sense of feel and not of sight. Second, the player's conscious mind must and will concern itself with some thought during the course of the action. Unless it is properly directed, almost invariably it will take notice of some single detail of the action, which will in consequence be overemphasized, to the detriment of the stroke as a whole.

Failure to recognize the first of these accounts for the practice of teaching the game by expounding it in theory. Detailed descriptions of different

119

phases of the stroke as made by experts are offered. It is a simple matter to describe with reasonable accuracy and clarity what a good golfer does so far as the eye can see. The teacher may go farther and show by example just how it is done, inviting the pupil's attention to such points as he may be trying to emphasize at the time. He may also display pictures of famous players in action, and show how their positions at varying stages of the stroke support his claims.

But unfortunately such a procedure more often than not falls short of conveying to the pupil the prescription he needs for his golf ills, for the plain reason that the pupil must learn from his own sense of feel and not from what he can see or visualize. Obviously, only the player himself can experience the feel of the thing. The problem is in a sense the reverse of the case of the blind men who went to "see" the elephant. The golfer can behold what a correct swing is in appearance, but for his own use he can know it only through feeling it.

Such a situation with regard to pupil and teacher, where failure to recognize this important fact exists, has led to much of the confusion that one hears reported by golfers who have taken lessons from several different teachers. It is quite a common thing to hear that one instructor taught one thing, while another taught something quite different, and even contradictory. Likewise in the long list of books written on the subject, one encounters a great many contradictions on moot points in the swing. Again, there are many other seeming contradictions, which appear to arise from unfortunate choice of language to convey an idea or in the interpretation of some certain action.

Through several years of editorial service with *The American Golfer*, I had frequent experiences of receiving letters from readers, asking how a statement in a recent article by some well-known expert was to be reconciled with something that had appeared in an earlier issue by another outstanding performer. On examination, it was frequently discovered that both writers had in reality had practically the same conception of the phase of the stroke involved, but their methods of explaining it varied so widely as to appear actually contradictory.

Let me illustrate how such a situation might arise. A few years ago, negotiations were in progress with a famous professional, internationally known for his play with iron clubs, for a series of articles dealing with that subject. Like most professional teachers, he was a ready and willing talker on the theories of the game, but balked at the thought of putting his ideas on paper. After considerable urging, he said, "Why don't you fellows go ahead and write the articles in the office; you know what my theory is. You just whip the club head through with the right hand."

I understood perfectly well the meaning he was trying to convey. He was simply giving expression to the feeling he experienced in striking the ball. The stroke with him was, of course, a swinging action, which picked up speed gradually, so that the club head attained its maximum pace at impact. This was the "pay-off" on what had already been built up, and at that particular instant, owing to the natural wrist action resulting from a swing, he experienced a feeling of flicking the club head through with his right hand.

But suppose we consider another possible interpretation of "whipping the club head through with the right hand," which might have led to another conclusion. Repeated articles in past issues of the magazine had pointed out the prevailing difficulties of a vast horde of players resulting from too vigorous use of the right hand. The subject of how the misapplication of power through the right hand will destroy a swinging action in the stroke, because of the introduction of leverage, has been fully discussed in these pages, so that no further comment is necessary. But it requires little imagination to understand how a reader of such an article, recommending that the player aim at "whipping the club head through with the right hand," might interpret it as a bold contradiction of the previous advice to subordinate the action of the right hand and arm to that of the left.

122

Another source of difficulty encountered by the golfer in trying to interpret suggestions and advice dealing with some detailed discussion of a single phase of the stroke lies in overemphasizing the action, and also in failure to realize that the action may be peculiar to the individual, or at least to players of a certain definite type. As a case in point, during the years that Bobby Jones was writing on the instructive side of golf, he commented from time to time on the importance of "getting the left hip out of the way" immediately after the downswing was begun.

It goes without saying, of course, that Jones had become an exceptionally fine golfer long before he was even conscious, so far as hitting a golf ball was concerned, that he had hips, or knew what they did during the swing. It was only in the later years, when he sought to analyze just what he did, that he gave any conscious thought whatever to just how his hips behaved during the swing. Eventually he came to notice that, when he was playing particularly well, his left hip appeared to turn away from the line of play immediately after he started the club down from the top. It was logical enough to catalogue this action as one of the things to be achieved. So long as a conscious reminder of the need for this did not interfere with the main business of swinging the club, it did no harm, and may have been a help.

But consider now the case of another player, who may have taken this pointer as the chief guide to keeping him on the track during the stroke. To do so, it will first be useful to check over certain facts relative to Jones's swing, and conditions that contribute to it. He is not very tall, is stockily built, and plays from a rather narrow stance. These conditions make for body action in his case which may be and actually is somewhat different from that of other types of players. The power in a golf stroke is supplied largely by the strong muscles of the legs and back. It is put into action by a shift of the center of gravity of the body, through leg action. It functions in a shift of the center of gravity toward the right on the upswing, and in reverse toward the left in the down stroke.

Almost coincidental with this shift comes a turning of the body, effected largely in the hip joints. This combined action finds varying degrees in the proportion of shift to turn in different types of players. The tall slender player requires a wider base, and is likely to employ a more noticeable shift, or lateral hip action. The short stocky one may shift very slightly, but makes up for the deficiency with a rotary hip turn. So with Jones. Almost from the time of starting the stroke, the hips begin to rotate toward the right.

On the down stroke, a reverse action toward the left takes place and in the same order. That is to say, if there is a perceptible lateral shift going back, it precedes the turning; likewise in the downswing. In the case of Jones, the shift is so slight that the turning begins practically at once. As a consequence, the left hip begins to swing back away from the line of play with the start down, which accounts for the sensation he experiences of "getting the left hip out of the way" at once.

If one who read this comment on hip action happens to conform fairly well to Jones's physical proportions, and for that reason can reproduce Jones's body action normally in swinging the club, such hip action on his part will be wholly consistent. If, on the other hand, there is any considerable difference in physical proportions, Jones's action would in all probability prove difficult for the other player, and an effort to effect it might easily prove a distinct physical handicap, even with a player who had already developed a swing. In any case, an effort to organize the stroke for the conscious purpose of pulling the left hip back away from the line charts a difficult course.

Coinage of well-turned phrases, in an effort to interpret the action in the stroke, may also lead to confusion. At one time in his career, a prominent professional of my acquaintance hit on the expression "Keep the weight back of the swing," as a means of inducing correct body action by his pupils. It may have proved helpful with some of them, particularly when employed by him, with physical demonstrations during personal instruction. But if one stops to ponder the advice, and to reason out just what it means, one may encounter complications and end in confusion.

His purpose was quite sound, as will appear when it is more fully explained along the following lines: It has been pointed out that the legs, through shifting the position of the middle part of the body at the hips, originate and set in motion the real power employed in the stroke. The muscles of the back contribute by completing the turn of the body necessary to allow the hands and arms to swing the club back. Since this locates the seat of the power, it also indicates where the power must be applied. In golf, as in throwing a baseball, delivering a punch in boxing, serving in tennis, and elsewhere, the weight of the middle of the body moves in the direction of the punch and moves ahead of it. Just how, therefore, could one expect to "keep the weight back of the swing" and still put in any real force into the stroke?

What this professional actually meant can be explained in the following analysis of the stroke: In making a full swing, the player turns his body as freely as possible. Because of applying the power at the center, as is necessary in a true swing, the body turn actually leads the action. The turn is accomplished chiefly in the hips, with some addi-

126

tional windup of the body above the hips. This
extra turn follows the turning at the hip joints. It
does so in the backswing, and it should do so in the
downswing. That is to say, the turning toward the
left at the hips should be practically completed
before the unwinding of the body above the hips
begins to take place. This hip action leads the
downswing, so that the weight of the middle of the
body has moved toward the left as the hands are
starting the club down, and therefore leads the
hands. This is contrary to the suggestion to "keep
the weight back of the swing."

The purpose intended in that phrase was to
induce the correct order in turning; that is, the hip
turn should take place before the unwinding of the
body above the hips is begun. He had had experience enough, no doubt, with a reversal of the order
by his pupils. What he had not seen and recognized
was that their failure was readily and easily
traceable to the fact that they were not in reality
swinging the club at all, but were employing leverage in the stroke from first to last. As a consequence
the free body turn, responsive to a swinging action,
was not taking place. They were not getting the
correct sequence, in the hip and upper body turning, going back, and neither were they attaining it
coming down. Introduction of leverage, through
misapplication of power with the right hand, caused
a turning of the shoulders in the start of the down-

127

swing. And this thrust with the shoulders the professional interpreted as getting the weight ahead of the swing.

This effort to convey an idea is so closely akin to another about which much has been written and spoken, "hitting from the inside out," that some comment on the latter would seem to be in order. Here again a pet phrase has been employed with the design of leading the player to bring about a swinging action, through visualizing what ought to take place from the top of the swing down to the ball.

We have only to go back and review briefly the action that takes place when the player swings to see how readily "hitting from the inside out" conforms with swinging. In case of a right-handed player, the left arm and hand constitute the guiding and directing factor in swinging, since the left hand is on the end of the club shaft. Hence the left arm will be fully extended throughout the action until the ball has been struck, establishing and maintaining, together with the shaft of the club, the radius of the swing. This implies that the right arm will be subordinated, and will drop naturally down by the right side as the club is taken back to the limit of the upswing.

Likewise, in swinging down, the left arm continues to guide the action as the hands start down. Because of the position assumed by the wrists in effecting the change of direction of the club head the latter is well behind the hands at this stage, as referred to the positions of the two agencies in the address. Again, the turning of the body above the hips follows the hips turn which begins with the start of the downswing, and the hands are well on their way down before this upper body turn is completed. This is the natural order in swinging. Obviously, therefore, unless there is interference, the hands and consequently the club head will be swung through on a horizontal arc, cutting the line of play at the ball. Furthermore, because of the swinging action, the pull of the club head outward will cause the left arm to remain extended.

In the foregoing circumstances, the hands and arms will swing through with the left shoulder extended upward, through a bracing of the left side, essential to maintaining a swinging action, and the right shoulder will swing down and under. Contrariwise, if the right hand and arm begin to introduce leverage into the stroke in starting the downward movement, by applying power between the left hand and the club head, left-arm control and direction of the stroke are destroyed. There is no longer an outward pull by the club head, and the expanding action of a swing is changed to a contracting one. This results in a drawing inward of the hands, thus altering the path of the club head, so that it no longer reaches the ball on an arc cutting the line of play at the ball, from the inside. Conversely right-hand domination and a conse-

129

quent lateral turn of the shoulders, beginning with the start of the downswing, will cause the club head to cross the line well back of the ball and to come to the ball on an arc cutting the line from the outside.

I have cited here a few typical cases of difficulties that are inevitably to be encountered where the teacher's effort at teaching and the pupil's attempt to learn the golf stroke fail to recognize the necessity for the latter to work through his sense of feeling the action. Lack of such recognition, as has been pointed out, leads to the numerous contradictions by teachers in their efforts to get their messages over to pupils. And what is very much more important, it leaves the pupil himself groping in the dark.

Now, lest someone confuse the foregoing examples of theorizing about the whys and wherefores of the stroke with what has been said in the earlier chapters of this volume with regard to paying no attention whatever to individual body functions, let me call attention to the fact that this is *theorizing,* and not an effort at practical teaching. It may appeal to your curiosity, but it is not likely to help your game. To that end, you are strongly commended to following closely what Ernest Jones has to say. He is a practical teacher, and an eminently successful one. Better string along with him.

ON THE SUBJECT OF
CONCENTRATION

WHEN a high-handicap player reads a story telling how some well-known expert soars into the high 80's with one or more 7's or an 8 on his card for a round, he may get a certain secret solace in realizing that golf can and does take its toll of high and low alike. But he is likely at the same time to marvel that such a thing can happen. It hardly seems possible when one recalls the steady machinelike precision with which the experts hit the ball in their normal stride.

How can such a lapse from form be explained? The same man swings the same clubs, but with such vastly different results. Moreover, he holds the club in the same way and stands to the ball in like manner on both occasions. He even indulges in the same mannerisms, so far as one can discern from watching him. There is no noteworthy change that one can see, unless by chance the observer is keen enough to note that the stroke is possibly hurried a bit. That would be one difference, but the important difference is not something that shows up readily in outward appearances.

In the preceding chapter, mention was made of the extreme importance of preventing conscious thought from interfering with the business of swinging the club during the stroke. Any number of things may flash across the player's mind to distract his attention. When the particular thought that engages his attention relates to a condition attendant on the stroke about to be played, it will almost surely interfere with the stroking. Hence, before any permanent improvement and progress can be made, the player must give consideration to training himself to shut out interference from this source.

It may be accepted as a definite truth that, when the experts are playing their best, they are actually conscious of nothing from the time the stroke is begun until the ball has been struck, except the sensation of swinging the club head. Note that this is true *when they are playing their best*. When they are playing badly, you also may set it down that, in practically every case, their troubles are due to conscious mental interference through thinking of something else.

Ordinarily this condition is referred to as lack of ability at the time to concentrate properly. Possibly that expresses it as well as any other statement. At any rate, I want to report here certain experiences that have come to my attention, as bearing out the foregoing.

Some years ago, Eddie Loos, a well-known and successful teacher, told of an experience he had had in giving lessons to a member of the club to which he was attached at the time. The two had been working together for several weeks with no appreciable success. Finally, in the course of one lesson, Loos informed his pupil that he had reached his wit's end in trying to help him, and that he honestly felt that any further effort was useless; it would be a waste of his time and the pupil's money and time.

They sat down on a near-by bench and lighted cigarettes as a gesture toward relieving the embarrassment that both of them felt. Eventually the pupil turned to Loos and asked, "Eddie just what do you think about when you are hitting the ball?"

Much to his astonishment, Loos admitted he could not say. After brief reflection, he said so far as he knew he didn't really think about anything, except hitting the ball. But the question prompted him to ask the pupil what *he* thought about.

"Well," he answered, "I try to think about taking the club back slowly, keeping my head still, keeping my left arm straight, making a full pivot,

133

and so on—all the things you have been telling me to do."

Without further comment Loos walked over to the practice tee, teed the ball, handed the pupil a club, and told him to step up to the ball and hit it, with no thought of any of the things he had mentioned—just hit it. The result was an agreeable surprise to both of them. It was a straight shot well down the fairway.

It would make a much better story to report that from that point on the pupil went on to become a first-rate golfer. As a matter of fact, he did not. He did improve, but Loos admitted that he learned a great deal more from that lesson than did the pupil.

It is a matter of very common knowledge, of course, that the strain of important championships, particularly those played on a stroke, or medal-play basis, takes its toll of even the most expert and the most experienced. A few years ago, the conclusion of an active winter campaign among the professionals, I checked up the winning scores in ten different events and compared them with the winning scores in the last ten Open Championships. It happened that there was a difference of a fraction more than nine strokes in the average scoring for the two sets of events.

Admittedly, the courses over which the ten independent tournaments were played were not so difficult as those chosen for the Open; yet this did not account in full for the discrepancy. Here, for example, is a case in point. Walter Hagen won the 1927 Western Open Championship over the No. 4 course of the Olympia Fields Country Club near Chicago with a four-round total of 281. The following year, the United States Open was played over that same course. Johnny Farrell and Bobby Jones tied for first place at 294, while Hagen himself was fifteen strokes higher than his winning total a year before.

This so-called tension is manifested for the most part in the failure of the player to keep his conscious mind from interfering with his habitual control of the club by subconscious direction. Realizing the importance of the event, there is a natural tendency to become tense, and tenseness destroys the easy rhythm of swinging or renders it very much more difficult. There is no more convincing testimonial to this effect in the records of important championships than was offered in the last nine holes of Al Espinosa's fourth round in the 1929 Open Championship at the Winged Foot Golf Club, near New York.

Espinosa began his final round three strokes back of Bobby Jones, who was setting the pace. By the luck of the draw Espinosa was playing about six holes ahead of Jones. He finished the first nine in 38, two over par, and very good golf under the conditions, but he probably did not expect it to reduce the disparity between his score and that of Jones. Yet there was always the chance that something might happen to Jones. Espinosa played the tenth and eleven in par 3 and 4, but at the twelfth, a par 5, he came to grief, eventually carding an 8. The reaction was nothing short of marvelous. He reasoned, logically enough, that he was through then and there, so far as winning the title was concerned. The pressure was off, so from there on he was merely playing out his string. True enough, there was still prize money in sight, but the prospect of winning was gone. In consequence, he proceeded to play the next six holes in a total of twenty-two strokes, two better than par. In the meantime Jones was having his troubles, and that dizzy pace that Espinosa, relieved of tenseness, set over the last six holes, put Jones in the position of having to hole a curling 12-foot putt on the home green to earn a tie.

More recently, the playing of Jones in the Masters' Open tournament at the Augusta National Golf Club early in April, 1936, afforded another very interesting observation on this same subject. In his four practice rounds prior to the competition, Jones was something like fifteen strokes under par for the seventy-two holes. Yet in the tournament he was well over par in each of the four rounds, with a difference of some twenty-five strokes between his total here and in the four practice rounds.

The mere fact that he played so brilliantly during practice was proof enough that there was nothing at all wrong with the muscular routine of his stroke. Incidentally, in one of these rounds he had a 64, the best card ever turned in for the course. That was well-nigh flawless golf in every department of play. No one plays such golf without superb control and mastery of the club. And only through smooth, steady stroking, as developed by a true swing, can such control be obtained. How else, then, can one account for the difference in his performance during the practice rounds and that in the actual competition other than by his mental state, which rendered it impossible to prevent conscious mental activities from interfering with his normal subconscious control during the stroke?

Another interesting case bearing on this matter was recorded in the experiences of Craig Wood during the winter campaign in California some three years ago. In this instance Wood won something like three out of four successive tournaments in which all the stellar performers of the winter circuit were engaged. For some time prior to that Wood had been recognized as a very fine player, capable of winning in any company. Yet at no other time had he maintained so long a stretch of consistently brilliant play. He was asked whether he had any theory or explanation as to why he had achieved such a record. He did have his own explanation, and made it. He explained that during his protracted spree of brilliant scoring he had purposely taken a brassie from the tee instead of a driver, and as a result he had succeeded in keeping the ball straight down the fairway with greater consistency than ever before.

Wood is strong and powerful, with mighty wrists and forearms, and he has an established reputation as a long hitter. It is also a notable fact that under observation he gives the impression of putting a mighty punch into the stroke just at impact, with a terrific whiplash action of the wrists. In other words, in appearance he is distinctly a "hitter" as contrasted with a "swinger." Expressed in other terms, in his case there is more of the show of leverage between the two hands, as the club head nears the ball, than is observed with most of the topnotchers.

In choosing a brassie, with slightly more loft, instead of a driver off the tee, Wood was making a mental concession to himself on the point of distance. Convinced that he could hit the ball far enough for any practical purpose with the brassie, he felt no urge to lash at it so furiously. The instinctive impulse to "put everything into it" just before impact was no longer present. And for this reason he quit "pressing," and relied on a normal,

138

free swing. The results were obvious in the fine scoring. This is further evidence that a mental condition which eliminates from the conscious mind all thoughts other than sensing a feel of swinging the club head is essential to control and consistency.

A veteran amateur of my acquaintance, who has been prominent in senior golf circles for some years, told me one of his experiences, which further emphasizes the importance of cultivating concentration, or the exclusion of conscious thought from interfering with the habitual swinging action. He had been off his game for several weeks, and appeared quite unable to get his swing properly adjusted. Then an idea occurred to him near the end of a match, in which he had been playing very badly.

"I decided," he said, "that maybe it was the old bugaboo of lifting my head that was causing all the trouble. So I made up my mind that over the last three holes, I would watch the ball until I hit it. I played the last three in par, and the next time I went out I found that all I had to do was just make sure that I looked at the ball, and my game came back as suddenly as it had left me."

Of course, he looked at the ball, but, what was much more important, he set his conscious mind to a simple task, which prevented it from concerning itself with numerous other details of what was wrong with his stroke. As a result, he escaped

139

interference from this source. His stroke normally was a swing unless it suffered interference, and, when he eliminated this by watching the ball, the ordinary and customary muscular routine that directed the stroke took charge and carried through.

Golf in this country has had few more interesting characters than Douglas Edgar, an English professional who came to this country shortly after the war and took a job in Atlanta, where he was killed in an automobile accident several years ago. He was accustomed to saying that he "thought the shot where he wanted the ball to go, and just hit it there." Expressed in another way, he framed a mental picture of striking the ball, stood in the position to hit at a certain objective, and then swung the club, with no thought of anything else.

Most of us cannot think the ball where we want it to go, because we think, not in terms of how we are swinging, but of how we are trying to strike the ball. We think of some detail of the striking, and not of the action of swinging. In this we encounter the greatest single obstacle to learning to play well. Our mental activities during the stroke are our greatest problem. It is not actually difficult to learn to swing the club head. The action of itself is quite simple. The trouble lies in restraining the mind from concerning itself with something that interferes with swinging. To avoid such trouble, set the conscious mind the task of thinking only of sensing a feel of a swing with the club head. This requires training and practice, but it is the surest means to the desired end in learning to play golf well.

Keeping conscious mental processes from interfering with subconscious control in the routine of wielding the club is true concentration in a golf sense.

YOUR GOLF AND YOUR EGO

GOLF is something more than a mere game. It is a religion. . . . And it exposes in a man things which ordinarily he is at considerable pains to conceal."

Thus wrote the late Walter J. Travis, after more than a quarter of a century of intimate contact with this very old game. As with most matters pertaining to the game, the great man was right. It appeals to all kinds and types of persons. And their reactions to the resistance it offers to their efforts to master it are interesting and sometimes extraordinary.

Since, as in all things, there must eventually come the striking of a balance between what the game yields and the price paid, it may be of interest to record certain of the phenomena, relating to

142

the plague of golfitis, which have come to my attention.

I recall the case of a successful writer who became keenly interested in the game some ten years or so ago. He is by nature quite logical and orderly in his consideration of any subject. After he had been playing for possibly two years, during which time he reached a stage where he was averaging around 90, he gave it calm reflection, and decided that there appeared no logical and plausible reason why he should not play consistently around par, if he but chose to give the time and effort necessary to do so. He resolved that he would.

He began a thorough study of the mechanics, and widened his reading to include books by several well-known players. He interviewed many famous professionals. He took pictures of expert players at varying stages of their strokes, until he satisfied himself fully that he knew just what had to be done to hit the ball straight and far. He went further. His home was located in a suburban town on the outskirts of New York, and fortunately he had space enough to permit him to practice short iron shots when he chose, even though he could not take a full wallop.

Meantime he was making the most of the time he had available for recreation by playing or practicing at a near-by course. And he made substantial headway. His scores came down into the middle 80's, eventually to the low 80's, with an occasional round in the high 70's. But there it hung. He visited different teachers and tried any and all kinds of tips, but none helped. Instead of making further improvement, he actually began to lose a part of what he had gained. But still the conviction that he should some day become able to play consistently at or near par was strong in him. He persistently plugged away in the vague hope that somehow or other it would come to him, overnight so to speak. But hope in the end died a horrid death.

He resolved to give up the game entirely and did. What is more, he wrote and had published in a prominent monthly magazine an article, condemning the game as positively vicious and abhorrent. He charged that it made liars and cheats of its followers; that it was a grossly selfish game, which caused men to neglect their businesses and to desert their families. He was all in favor of a law patterned after the ancient Scottish edict of the fifteenth century, proclaiming that the game be "nicht usit and utterly cryit doun."

It was my misfortune to miss the article at the time of its publication, and it was only through the good offices of the author that it finally came into my hands some three years later. "I'll send a copy of the magazine over to you," he told me in the course of a telephone conversation, "if you would like to read it." I assured him that I would, whereupon he added, "But maybe you will be interested to learn that I got out the old bag two or three months ago, and am at it all over again."

Some three years ago, a prominent New York broker began a course of instruction under a famous instructor, whose system of teaching appealed strongly to him. His friends heard about it and indulged in some rather jeering comment at his expense. As a result, he made several wagers that within one year from that time he would have played at least six rounds under 80. His average score at the time was around 90 or slightly under.

Urged on by the determination to prove his contention with regard to the system of teaching, and likewise to collect from his cronies, he went to work in earnest. And the word "work" is chosen with deliberation. I watched him in several indoor practice sessions, and these were anything but play. With collar, tie, and shirt removed, he labored like a section hand, as the perspiration rolled off of him. And he won his bets.

A few years ago I spent a few days in the home of a prominent physician, who had been working like a trouper for more than a year to develop his stroke after a certain pattern. His wife informed me that he had been working much harder at golf during that period than he had at his profession. At that particular time he was still quite

145

puzzled over what he felt to be the lack of correct wrist action just prior to and at the moment of impact. The night I arrived he brought out a well-thumbed copy of a magazine article discussing this phase of the game, and we discussed it thoroughly.

On the following day we played golf, and he began to add considerable distance to his long shots, but, when it came to the shorter ones, he still experienced trouble in getting his wrists to function as he thought they should. That night we went back again to the magazine article, and the last thing I saw of him before retiring he was standing in the middle of the floor of the living room, swinging a mashie.

He had arranged an appointment at a hospital some two hours away to perform an operation at 9 o'clock the next morning, and it was agreed that we would get an early start. When I came down for breakfast, there he stood in the middle of the living room again, swinging that mashie. We finally parted shortly before 9, after he had had a call made to the hospital saying that he would be a couple of hours late in arriving as he had been delayed by an emergency operation!

Some time ago a personal friend of mine was invited to visit friends of his in an adjoining state to New York, with the plea that he should not fail to come. The message was from the lady of the household. On his arrival, he learned that he was to intercede with the lord and master to dissuade the latter from demolishing a sun porch on one side of the house. His purpose to do this was to improve one of three short pitch-and-putt holes he had built on the premises, because he felt that by so doing he could make it a much more interesting hole. In an uneven battle of two against one, he grudgingly gave way to superior forces.

There lately passed to his final reward a veteran player in one of the Eastern states, who astounded his friends one day with the announcement that on his 23,939th stroke he had made a hole in one. He claimed to have kept an actual record of every score he had made since he first took up the game many years before. He was a man of truthful habits, and there was no reason for questioning his accounting, even though one might marvel at the attention to detail which prompted him to keep such a record.

The foregoing are not revealed here as warnings to the reader of the peculiar eccentricities that the game may develop in its followers, or of the capricious mastery it may exercise over some of them. At the same time, it is suggested that one may well go into a quiet session with oneself and inquire just what one expects to get out of golf and what one is willing to pay for it. For one thing, temperament is a very important factor to be considered in attempting to teach the game.

One capable and intelligent teacher of my acquaintance always makes it a point to devote the
first lesson with any pupil to a somewhat rambling
conversation, in which mention of golf plays only
a casual part. He finds that these talks often give
him an insight into the player's manners, habits,
and reactions to different situations. Some are
nervous and high strung, eager, and anxious. Others
are disposed to become discouraged easily. Still
others affect a pose of not taking the game seriously, although a little adroit questioning may
reveal that they would almost barter their souls
for a winning game.

Less than a year ago, I stood talking in his shop
with a promising young professional; he suggested
that we go out to the practice tee where I could
watch him hit a few shots, to see whether I could
tell what was wrong with his swing. He hit four
or five balls, and every shot split the middle of the
fairway and traveled around 240 yards.

"Now that's funny," he said. "Yesterday I played
in a four-ball match with Jim, Mack, and George,
and I hooked every tee shot during the round.
Why do you suppose that was?"

I suggested that he might have had a few bets
on the match, and he admitted that he had.
Furthermore, the natural rivalry among the four
of them was quite keen. The other three were all
long-hitting young amateurs, who could give him

a good match when he started them one up on each side, as he usually did. The whole trouble in his case was overeagerness. He is by nature a nervous young man, as fidgety as a water bug. He cannot get up to the ball quick enough to play his next stroke. There was nothing whatever to criticize in the way he swung the club there on the practice tee.

A veteran player of my acquaintance tells me that he has for many years approached the first tee with one firm resolution—to take it easy for the first three holes; not to expect too much, but rather to feel that he is likely to hit a few bad shots until he finally begins to get the feel of the thing. Such a practice leaves him resigned to a few bad ones, if he does hit them, and avoids stirring up mental kinks, which might easily interfere with his play for the full round, not only adding extra strokes to his score but cutting sharply into the full enjoyment of his day's fun.

There is no reason why anyone with ordinary physical qualifications cannot learn to play golf reasonably well, given the opportunity to approach it in a sensible and intelligent way, and assuming that he is willing to give the time and effort necessary to practice. Not all can or will develop the same degree of skill with the same amount of effort. Some have more natural aptitude than others, better muscular coordination, a fuller

149

capacity for acquiring the right kind of concentration on the stroke, and so on.

Yet, to a considerable extent, in all cases one gets out of the game what one puts into it. And that includes the manner in which one goes about applying one's effort. It is obviously of vast importance to learn in the easiest way, because the easiest way pays the highest dividends for the effort expended. The early chapters of this volume are devoted to explaining as fully as possible the method Ernest Jones employs in his teaching. It is a simple, positive, and direct method, and he has achieved very fine results with it. It most surely is worthy of the full consideration of all those who seriously want to play golf well.

CPSIA information can be obtained at www.ICGtesting.com
Printed in the USA
LVOW11s0840120315

430111LV00002BA/218/P